Praise for

Voices in the Vines

'It is as if the writer has opened readers' eyes to a momentary sight, and we dwell on it as long as the writer allows, hopeful it may not disappear when we blink'.

Professor Graeme Harper, editor of *New Writing: International Journal for the Practice and Theory of Creative Writing*

'Throughout the book the author's voice is delightfully light and humorous, but the final message is one that will move you and make you think.'

Valerie Mobley, Society of Editors, Australia

As the author of this work I acknowledge the Traditional Custodians of the Kaurna Yerta, and pay my respects to Elders past, present and emerging.

VOICES IN THE VINES

Voices in the Vines

Roy Neill

CPH

Cove Publishing House LLC

First published in 2022 by Cove Publishing House LLC

Publishing Manager: Counter Space

33 Pirie Street Adelaide, South Australia

https://www.counterspace.com.au/Voices

Cover design: Akiko Chan

ISBN 978 0 646 84133 5

To the memory of Norm and Norma Walker who invited us into their lives. To Norm who cast a long shadow in his lifetime; I was blessed to know you.

I am the present and the future of your children;
I am the memory of your past.

Maia Evele' Neill, 2009

1

Place

I bought a house and it told me a story. And the story becomes many stories that build a *place*. The stories are bricks, the mortar is people, and history is the scaffolding. The scaffolding is vast, stretching across time and in need of repair in places, but the bricks are sound and the mortar is true and the builder has used a blueprint. So let's go to this place; together we will examine the bricks, test the mortar, and inspect the scaffolding.

2

It's only got one bathroom

One hundred and sixty five thousand: something must be wrong with it.
'Why is it only one sixty-five?' I ask the agent.
'You do know it's only got one bathroom,' she huffed.

It has a foyer, a lounge room, three bedrooms, a family room, and kitchen with dinette, three open fireplaces, two toilets and, yes, one bathroom. Her words transport me to a house where I lived as a boy:

one sleep-out, two bedrooms, one sitting room, a dining room, a lean-to kitchen, one long-walk, long-drop toilet in the backyard, one laundry and, yes, one bathroom, also in the back yard—one open fire-place plus four chip heaters for cooking, washing clothes, and bathing two adults and seven children.

I smile at her and join the others in the strange silent dance of home inspection:

Promenade in the passage, look up at the walls, duck in and duck out, pirouette in the hall, make room for another to stand where you stood sniffing for dampness and knocking on wood. Continue the dance from room to room, excuse me beg your pardon, awkward looks in the loo. Poke fingers in a crevice on the lounge room wall, stroke plaster and salt damp at the end of the hall. And when it is over and the looking is done, the dancers determine what its fate will become (Neill 2010).

Worn shagpile carpets, a *cool* royal blue loo and chipped paint present a décor that blends late-neglect with early 'Austen Powers'. Along the passage and inside each room floorboards groan beneath my weight then moan a relieved thank you as I move on. But the walls are solid and the ceilings are high and it's easy to imagine how the place could look. It is rich with character and future possibilities. Echoes of other children's voices ring in the hallway. *How many grew tall in its shelter?* It feels like a home; it feels right.

The outside is quaint and old. Its roof sags under the weight of time and from the front it looks a little depressed: *perfect.* The free-stone walls are rough and craggy like the face of an old man, and rivulets of earthquake scars criss-cross the concrete on the porch. The moss-tinged roof bends and dips low over leadlight windows that peek from under the eaves at the intrusion in the garden.

Red blazers mobilize.

We gather at the front. I look around for the owners and my eyes settle on a huddle in the driveway. A group of people circle a man and a woman who are sitting on canvas chairs and holding hands. The woman's face and neck are flushed against her fair complexion. She chirps merrily away, drawing tiny circles in the air with a plump finger to make her point. The man sits low in his chair. He looks big and affable, and his long legs are at full stretch. His feet cross at the ankles in size ten boots that pulse like metronomes as he talks on his mobile phone.

'Good afternoon ladies and gentlemen. On offer today, a splendid example of a bygone era here in beautiful Magill ...'

The auctioneer's voice becomes staccato pops of speech lost in the rapids of traffic on Penfold Road.

'Close ... Penfolds ... winery ...'

Boom-boxes and sub-woofers in cars with exhaust pipes the size of cannons, conspire with titanic quarry trucks, whose drivers are hell-bent on punching a hole in the sky just above the horizon, to drown him out.

'You can ... a window ... grape ...'

A bouncy woman with frizzy fringe and red blazer dodges and weaves her official hips through the crowd and clip-clops onto the porch. She cups a hand around her puckered red mouth and hisses into the auctioneer's ear. He shakes and shivers and his knee jerks as he sucks air in sporadic gulps. With the bellows full he thunders ... 'CAN YOU HEAR ME NOW?' Polite hand claps told him we could. Two women stand close to me in the middle of the lawn. One is talking softly, and affectionately stroking the heads of two small children who cling to her colourful dress. The other woman is coiled, like a runner in the blocks waiting for the gun. Her hair is pulled back severely, removing all lines from her face. She wears a pin-striped man suit and constantly fidgets.

Behind the women stands a tall man with a striking thatch of tight white curls that spring from his scalp. Beneath the curls his eyes twinkle in a generous, ruddy smile which folds to a curious grin as the auctioneer continues.

'Can we have a number please, to get us started?'

'Fifty thousand,' snaps a voice. Astonished heads seek-out the perpetrator. The 'number' came from the pursed lips of a middle-aged man sporting an orange tan and a shimmering white jumpsuit draped in gold.

It is not the number the couple in the driveway had in mind. The agent's jaw muscles pulse under taut skin: he all but throws his gavel at the bidder.

'Ladies and gentlemen,' he schmoozes, 'we can do better than that, surely.'

The silence is uncomfortable as the seconds drag by. The circle of support in the driveway begins to unravel. Then the number one hundred thousand floats across the garden, and we are off and running.

The bidding comes down to the women standing near me. The one with the children continues to stroke them lovingly. They are now emotional decoys in the game. The other woman is all-business where motherly cooing is an alien emotion.

All-business makes a bid.

'Going once ... going twice ...'

I decide it is time and raise my forefinger to the sky.

'We have a new bidder,' cries a happy auctioneer.

One weary mother and two snarling children are now glaring at me. But all-business sticks out her chest and wobbles a bid which is quickly countered by a wiggle from mother-of-two.

'Going once ... twice ...'

I raise my forefinger to the sky. Mother-of-two shakes her head and silently gathers the children close. I feel bad. But all-business looks fierce; she crouches in my direction and hisses another bid.

'Going once … the bid is with you sir … going twice …'

I raise my forefinger to the sky. All-business growls, revealing unusually long canines. I swallow as she reaches beneath her coat. She flicks open a phone, like a switchblade, and talks while she walks.

After a dramatic final call, the auctioneer swings the gavel in a spectacular arc that ends in a dull thud in the palm of his hand. 'SOLD,' he cries, 'to the man in front … congratulations sir you have just bought a house.'

∞

Six weeks later the floorboards sing a welcome as we set furniture down and hang pictures up. We search the cupboards, sit on the floor, drink coffee and laugh at the way the high ceilings make us look small. I find ancient wine labels pasted in a cupboard, and discover archaic documents and old photographs of the *young* house when it was surrounded by grapevines.

And in a narrow frame above a fireplace, scantily clad cherubs, with curls and wings and quivers with arrows, play gleefully around the letters in the word 'Chickerloo'.

3

Procession of noise

The remnants of a strong gully breeze unfold like invisible hands over the treetops, urging the soft foliage into a gentle sway. The breeze loops and curls and dips low, disturbing the undergrowth, tumbling the dry leaves of summer. Its long tail twists from the vents in the hillsides that channel its course along the fork in the road that leads to the village. Up high again, it caresses the sheen of a billowing Southern Cross above the old hotel and then snaps the flag to its full glory before dropping to earth once more. Silently, it slithers over the road, twirling dust and paper in its wake, past the café where I sit and watch the street.

Up at the school cloistered schoolchildren are chaperoned by parents, grandparents, or older brothers and sisters. They arrive on foot or in cars that lurch and brake and beep and stagger to the drop-off point, and are then fed safely into the schoolyard. They pad by in a little league of nations: their roots in Great Britain, Ireland, Greece, Italy, India, Malaysia, Spain, Africa and the Middle East. But their collective futures are in Asia, they are told, so the only foreign language on offer in the curriculum of this school is Chinese.

At the crossroads a frantic jumble of cars, trucks, and buses are being spliced and separated by traffic lights: red is stop, green is go and amber is *go as fast as you can*. Drivers on red wait with unconcealed contempt for those on green. While the stragglers, who catch amber, lunge through the intersection with abandoned urgency before those on red get green, take aim, and propel their vehicles at the panic-stricken tailenders. Somehow it all works.

Aggression is the key. Empowered by automatic transmission and feather-touch steering, the elderly, the middle-aged and the young have equal rights in the fray. Countless cars fly by—one for every second of every minute of every hour of every day. There are more vehicles than people. Freedom once meant owning a car; now we are enslaved by them. Freedom in the future will belong to those who can get by without one.

Heavy trucks, carrying tonnage that could suffocate a small city, hammer a pathway past the school to and from the quarries at Stonyfell. Drivers sit high in their cabins above the roar of engines; brakes hiss, trays clang and drive shafts whine as drivers maraud down through thirteen gears to jerk the steel mammoths to a hesitant stop at the school crossing. Our tribes were not made for this. We were made for the peace and tranquillity of leafy glens, not this procession of noise. It makes us cranky and reckless.

A distant memory, trapped in the digital chimes of the school bell, demands order. And in a brief eerie stillness that follows, yellow and green-clad little people filter into classrooms as the breeze's tattered fingers ruffle their hair and tug at their clothes.

Traffic and food dominate the village of 21st-century Magill. On Magill Road a pizza man arranges chairs and tables in front of his tiny shop. He looks up as a schoolboy runs by. The boy has left his hat at the bus stop and the pizza man calls out to alert him. But the schoolboy is hard-wired to his iPod and hears nothing—so for today, no hat, no play.

The pizzeria heads a veritable street-buffet of indulgence that caters for all tastes. An obsession with food and a capacity to consume in large quantities has created a staggering assortment: Italian, Chinese, Indian, Thai, Greek, Subway, more Italian, Kitty's Sweet Treats, Red Rock noodle bar, plus a supermarket, a butcher, a baker and a roast chicken maker. It is a gourmet cluster, each a whiff away from the next. Exotic saffron-coloured aromas and the crackling allure of hot chip-fat meld in the street. I catch a scent that transports me in time; something from the past I cannot quite grasp a hold of. The fragrant air makes resistance futile. Dim Sims fry and drunken noodles slush and wobble in protest beneath the clumsy stabbings of chop-sticks, only to be caught and slurped into the dark grotto above. Heady smells of tangy marinara sauce, gooey mozzarella and rich, thick espresso mingle and seep through walls and windows and waft under doors. All around, bread bakes, chips fry, fat chickens roast, and curries churn. Behind the shops and restaurants, bins reek of discarded food. Nearby, people dine alfresco, only a whiff beyond the smell of fetid waste. We could feed the inhabitants of a third-world country with what is thrown away.

On television, food entertains us. Celebrity chefs convince amateur cooks that food is the only meaning to life—that through food they can achieve bliss and reach gourmet nirvana—then reduce them to tears when their efforts are dashed on the lick of a spoon. The abundance of food is mocked with televised food fights. Not just in children's programs, but in commercials where grandma and grandpa, who once chastised 'Think of all the starving children in India', flick mashed spuds smothered in cheese sauce at one another, and pack each other's wrinkles full of raspberry coulis. Mum and dad are there too. Up to their armpits in spaghetti bolognese, and it's still not clear exactly what is being sold.

Meanwhile children go hungry.

With food comes fat. Overindulgence has caused a pandemic of obese people. We watch how food is cooked then change channels to watch sad and pained souls, red-faced and drenched in perspiration, in a mazurka of weight loss—a ridiculous paradox of our times.

The smell of rich Italian espresso lures me from the street.

In the café four buoyant middle-aged women sip wine and coffee, eat cake and pizza, chew, chatter and trawl iPhone apps all at the same time. One of the women covers her mouth with her hand as she eats. It is not that she chews with her mouth open; it's as though she is embarrassed to be eating at all—*perhaps no one will notice*: the curse of the modern woman and her preoccupation with food and weight. Another woman rocks to and fro over her plate, encircling it protectively with her arms. Suddenly, the front door yawns and the wind sweeps a young woman inside. She wedges the door open with her behind while hitching her shopping bags into the crook of one arm. She glides across the floor, cradling the delicate form of a newborn baby in her other arm. The four well-fed women fall silent. Their faces show reverence, wonder and solidarity: coffee, cake, and apps forgotten.

The café owner knows the young mother. They softly hum and coo in a ritual of close, sisterly familiarity over the small swaddle of love. Fascinated, I watch the scene. But there is no peripheral eye contact in this encounter. So I take my coffee and head back to the street.

Outside, a denim-clad rider sits astride a Harley Fat Boy. He goads and guides the bike between two rows of stationary cars, running a gauntlet of side-mirrors. He grins in toothless triumph, having left some of them still intact. The lights change and he is gone in a blur of long hair, bruising tattoos and legs in long stirrups. The deafening roar of the bike's unbridled exhaust sounds like the repeated retorts of a combat rifle. It seems that when parading your persona, the loudest attracts the most attention and therefore wins.

Asian students chatter and giggle and twitter and google as they stroll by beneath a thick carpet of glossy black hair. Their eyes are fused to iPhone and iPod screens. They emanate a religious air of prayer and mantra at the glassy altar of the idol. One beautiful young woman pecks repeatedly at her keypad. Her dark-red fingernail is the beak of a delicate bird urging the worm in the icon to reveal its wonders.

The deadly hum of a motorised granny-buggy splits the group. Etched in expressions of a lifetime, granny's face contorts to resemble Popeye. Asserting her arthritic rights, she ploughs through them, venting her pent-up wrath with a shrill flag-flapping cackle and extended blasts on the buggy-horn. The group gives way, and then folds in fits of laughter. Perhaps her grandson has a Harley Fat Boy.

At the bus stop, a heavy-set man rolls his shoulders and shuffles aggressively towards commuters gathered in the shelter. He growls at them, asking for money. His face is wine-red, broad and wolf-like. Blossoms of purple veins swathe his pulpy nose. Whiskery stubble traces his jaw, and dark looks trace his eyes. They dart from face to face as the wind whips thin strands of his hair into a Medusa halo. Two young boys, an elderly woman, and a man in a dark, tight-fitting business suit sit in awkward silence, looking away. A shockingly tall, black schoolgirl chews gum as she leans against the corner of the shelter, her presence stark and vivid in this setting. Her skin is so black it reflects light. Her elegant features lose definition in her aura, which is the colour of midnight. She has high cheekbones, full lips and dark, knowing eyes; her face a mix of pride and dignity. She is not an indigenous Australian; indigenous Australians are all but absent on the streets of Magill. The girl is from the local Sudanese community.

She stares blankly ahead as the beggar's gaze singles her out. She slings her schoolbag over her shoulder and moves gracefully into the shade of a nearby tree. The beggar's gaze pierces the space between them, but she refuses to connect. Another man, with bat-like ears that protrude from beneath a construction worker's hard hat, shouts incoherently at the beggar. The man is distressed and his face shows a frightened, child-like concern. He is not a construction worker; he is from the nearby home for men in need. His days in Magill are spent pacing the footpath, wearing his hat in a different world. A serpentine smile splits the beggar's face and he slinks away.

The passengers board the bus. As it leaves, a black face appears through the dust on the rear window; the schoolgirl smiles to the man in the hard hat.

In the supermarket car park a young male shopper struggles to unlock his car. His mobile phone is tucked under his chin and he juggles a large pack of toilet rolls, two bottles of soft drink, a newspaper and a jumbo pack of Tim Tam biscuits. In a contorted effort to reach his car keys, he claws desperately at the pocket in the back of his track pants. The track pants are a strange array of multi-coloured triangles and panels, reminiscent of early Jackson Five, and they hang very low in the crotch. He swears and bends to pick-up the phone that has now fallen from beneath his chin, only to expose the creases that form the 'Y' between his milk-white buttocks—a possible source of the name for his generation.

His gyrations and curses amuse two middle-aged women in the adjoining parking space. They giggle and whisper behind their hands at his lack of fashion sense and overall helpless maleness. The two women place their neatly packed shopping bags in the back of a 'big-end Beamer' and disappear with a breakneck surge of speed. Middle-aged women in invincible 4-wheel drives, with windows tinted covert-black, have introduced new dimensions of terror to the roads.

I watch two young African males. One is tall and athletic while the other is short and solidly built. The shorter of the two leans lazily against one of the verandah posts in front of the chip shop. He looks distracted. Posturing, he studies his fingernails while affirming his presence by talking loudly and rapidly into his mobile phone. Snatches of the conversation are in English 'That's his swag, bro' and 'Not if I can help it, he won't'. I am an uninvited third party to this conversation. I find myself piecing together the subject matter from small grabs of English woven with his native tongue. Rightly or wrongly, I assess the character of the young man based on what I can hear.

Both men are dressed from head to toe in brightly-coloured designer clothing. Other than me, no-one seems to notice them. Their postures, and the determined way in which they hold their heads to maintain exclusive facial contact, indicate that they have set themselves apart: on a stage, so to speak, wanting to be noticed. They are a dazzling spectacle in this supermarket car park catwalk, where bizarrely-patterned happy pants, baggy track suits, Ugg boots[1] and thongs[2] are considered fashionable shopping attire. I continue to observe them in a bid to connect, but without success. They are now as locked into their roles in this scene as are those around them.

A gaunt, angular man with a bushy Ned Kelly[3] beard walks blindly by. With one hand he eats a pasty from a paper bag. The other hand holds his mobile phone as he studies the screen. His forehead is furrowed above his nose. His eyes squint in agitation at the glare. Flakes of pastry are caught in the briar of coarse hair around his mouth. The beard makes it impossible to tell his age. It could be any-where from twenty to forty. His arms are encased in cadaver-blue tattooed sleeves that cover all flesh to the wrists. I must have grimaced. He glares at me; I fake a smile. He maintains eye contact and digs his heels hard into the ground, stepping wildly and widely side-to-side as he passes aggressively by. It works. His appearance disturbs me. It reads, *avoid me at all costs.*

We live in hazardous times. Young men build their physiques to distended proportions lifting weights in the gym. For some it is the *look*: the six packs, the abs, and the broad shoulders; good for 'pea-cocking'. For others, it is self-preservation in a dangerous world, where alcohol-fuelled violence can deliver a single cowardly blow from out of the darkness, leaving young men dead in the streets—young men who look like easy targets to the soulless snipers. What's more, enlightened 21st-century justice often deems such violent attacks to be worth less gaol time than white-collar crimes. And these legal outcomes leave little for the snipers to weigh up in the way of conse-quences.

'You wouldn't have 60 cents, would you?'

The words are clipped and precise. I turn to look up at an enor-mous woman. Her face is plump and round with a sweaty sheen. There is more than a hint of body-odour and her expression is that of a young child caught doing something wrong. The mismatched clothing speaks of hard times. A short-sleeved, Spanish-style blouse hangs low over her pendulous breasts. The flesh beneath her upper arms jiggles as she sways nervously back and forth.

'I beg your pardon?'
'Have you got 60 cents?' She repeats, crisply enunciating each word.
An elasticised cotton skirt is hiked up at her waist, held up by providence over a protruding stomach. A sad-looking pink flower decorates her hair, which is bunched high in a bun on top of her head.

She is the 'faded rose' from some heart-rending country song. I don't have any change, but I plunge my hand into the front pocket of my jeans all the same. After rummaging around for effect, I mumble, 'Sorry'. She walks away without a word, approaches another man, and repeats her request. He plunges his hand into his pocket and comes up with some gold coins. She takes far more than sixty cents from his hand and walks away without a word. To ask for only 60 cents seems like a good strategy. Almost anyone will look for and part with 60 cents in small change. And if not 60, she will at least get something. I look in mild disbelief at this woman, begging in the streets in an age of plenty.

I trundle into the supermarket, unable to shake the habit I have developed lately of looking for faces from my past. *Where have all those people gone?* Fleeting, slightly embarrassed half-smiles and the occasional nod of the head from men of my generation is the only human contact as I walk the aisles. In the toiletries section a tiny Italian lady shuffles along in front of me. A black shopping bag hangs from her walking frame. One corner of her delicately crocheted black shawl trails the floor behind her. Black stockings hang in folds around her ankles and her feet are stuffed into white towelling bathroom slippers. She is craggy and bent and old and her hair is thin on top. While she can see and reach the goods on the lower shelves, the curvature of her spine prevents her from seeing or reaching anything barely above the second shelf. I stop and ask her if she needs help 'Ye-sa, of cour-sa...I'm a...nee-da...el-pa', she replies, surprised that I needed to ask at all. She hands me a scrap of paper. It is a shopping list written in clear, concise English. *She's come prepared to be helped.* I begin looking.

There is a commotion coming from the direction of the deli counter. I move closer. Cheese and olives and cold cuts of meat compete for selection alongside a disciplined rank of roast chickens with golden breasts and rounded thighs.

A robust, red-faced man with a ramrod-straight military look and wide, intense eyes stands at the front of the counter. He has a small brown dog tucked under his arm. The dog is wearing 'doggie duds', that is, a small fur-lined coat encircles his neck but exposes his rear—essential, I would think, for interaction in the world of dogs. The man gestures wildly, using the dog to point with. Suddenly he raises his voice: 'HE'S NOT GAY, BUT THE BLOKE HE SLEEPS WITH'S BROTHER IS.' He then directs a foamy spray of loud laughter in the direction of a young girl behind the counter—nodding his head to indicate the joke is now finished and she can join his laughter. Customers clutching next-to-be-served number slips look either annoyed or uncomfortable. Some stare blankly at the floor while others fix their eyes on points distant. From what I can tell, the man is either deaf or he has Tourette's syndrome. A woman beside me whispers with clandestine authority 'It's a hearing dog.'

I consider the marvels of the modern world for a moment. In the 1950s it was predicted that by the end of the twentieth century the world would be free of illness and disease and technology would be such that footpaths would be conveyer belts—much like those in major airports. There would be no need for roads because transport would be airborne: cars would fly—or was that pigs? But here we are well into the 21st century and man still relies on the creatures we share the planet with. I look at the man and his dog and wonder how the dog warns its master when he is telling a bad joke. *I imagine it wriggles or vibrates its tiny body, much like a mobile phone in silent mode.* I look at the young shop assistant. She smiles politely at the man and his dog. She does not laugh. His joke is out of its time. Humour changes with the generations.

The incident slowly ebbs away as waiting customers give a mental hurry-up to those being served ahead of them. They fidget and fold and unfold their arms, and turn in small obsessive circles looking at expensive delicacies that they won't be buying today.

Children wearing the green and yellow uniforms of the Magill primary school are gathered in front of the sweets and treats displays. They wring their hands and point and laugh. They plead with one another for help with the excruciating array of choices. The children are as colourful as the treats on display: a mix of nationalities. One small boy wears what I guess to be a Sikh turban. It looks like a sock knotted on top of his head. The headwear would have brought him untold misery in the schoolyards of Australian society a few short years ago. Today, however, it goes almost unnoticed, especially by other children. In them there is much hope for the future. Two of the group have Asian characteristics. I listen, captivated as they talk with accents that are so perfectly Australian. I have lived in Australia most of my life and still have an Irish accent. When asked why, I usually say I couldn't find a better one. But I think subconsciously I maintain it partly in defiance of the mockery from those early years as a migrant, but mostly because it keeps me connected to who I am and where I'm from.

The check-out operators (COOS) are dealing as best they can with the pay-week deluge of food shoppers (FOOS). They smile and nod and bleep gargantuan quantities of foodstuffs across a barcode sensor. The daily script is unchanged as the production lines file through:
COOS: 'How are you?'
FOOS: 'Good thanks.'
COOS: 'Any fly-buys?'
FOOS: 'Yes.'
COOS: 'Cash out?'
FOOS: 'No.'
COOS: 'Thank you; have a good day.'

The express lane is choked with FOOS who have many more than the obligatory 12 items. I think of espresso coffee and the coffee-making machine invented so commuters could catch the express train and still have a good cup of coffee. This express lane is quicksand. I stare at the headlines of a glossy magazine while I wait: 'TOO FAT TO FLY … SO I LOST 100 kg!' *Well, she should be able to generate some lift now.*

I leave the supermarket and walk outside. The sky is now a pewter-coloured quilt spread above the hills. Some of the clouds are shredded candy-floss strands that trail down the hillsides, showing vivid blue through fissures. Others are bruised and heavy with moisture. The air is warm—warm enough to rain.

I am invisible on this street: eye contact is avoided at all costs. Perhaps it is me—my look, my age, my generation. Many passers-by seem cocooned, blinkered and impossible to read. All about me faces are fastened to mobile phone screens. I leave the street as the first drops of rain slap the ground and dissolve in warm patches of sunlight, and the words of a song fill my head:

Looks like we're all alone together
That's not the way it's meant to be
Can't even talk about the weather
I don't see you—you don't see me

It feels so strange like falling with the rain
Lying in a puddle
My life's a haze moving in a daze
Through an empty tunnel

No need to smile no need to look no need to care
All alone inside a pod is anybody out there …

Song lyrics, Neill 2006©

4

It was not that long ago

'Makgill' began as a 524-acre estate that lay in the long shadows
beneath the stringybark forests of the Mount Lofty ranges in South
Australia. Two Scotsmen, Robert Cock and William Ferguson, were
granted the land in 1837 and they built a farmhouse in the space that
would become Penfold's Grange Hermitage vineyard. Hard times
forced Cock and Ferguson to sell their estate. In a push for cash, an
80-acre plot at the northern end of their holding was divided and sold
as village allotments and small farms. Named in honour of David
Maitland Makgill, the Cock family trustee in Scotland,[4] the village of
Makgill came into being. But a name becomes a place and with time
the stilted pronunciation of the brittle Scottish 'k' in Makgill, gave way
to euphony and the pleasant-sounding 'Magill.'

Magill was a successful founding in anyone's language, unless you
were one of the native inhabitants. Where the natives were was where
the Europeans wanted to be. The Kaurna people inhabited the land
alongside continuously flowing spring-fed creeks and their inevitable
displacement became a quiet acquiescence to the frenetic drive of the
settlers.

Progress was swift. Magill became a Mecca for travellers making
their way inland from the port, and a crossroads for fruit growers and

loggers who delivered their wares west to the city of Adelaide and beyond.

Christopher Rawson and Mary Penfold built a cottage where Ferguson's farmhouse had been, and called their home 'The Grange' after a cottage in Scotland owned by a Holt family friend, Rob Roy McGregor. Vine cuttings from France, Italy and Spain were planted beneath a vast Australian sky of pristine light. The place was ideal for growing fruit, with warm days, cool nights and rich fertile soil.

In time grape vines covered the foothills alongside thriving orchards of apples, pears and olives. And in 1846 the botanist Charles Giles created a garden of wonder at the source of Third Creek, where he planted every flower and tree catalogued in the known world at the time.

The village grew: a schoolhouse, police station, post office and butcher's shop shared the main street with a smugglers' snug and a workingman's pub. Mansions and cottages were built reflecting every strata of established society. Your rank in the strata was determined by your measure of wealth and your ownership of land. But rich and poor alike shared the essential beauty of the place: your rank in the strata would never change that.

Magill was a predominantly Scottish enclave, of doggedly faithful religious men and women, who built their places of worship as solidly as their faith, to stand the test of time. For the sick, the old and the needy, and for those who lived at society's margins, came the institutions. At the quaint extreme the old folks' home cared for the elderly while the Lentara children's home sheltered orphaned and abandoned children. But at its harshest extreme the dark cloak of institution concealed the misery of those who bore the label of 'destitute and criminal children'. And hidden behind brownstone walls, beneath the misty title of 'Reformatory School', nine boys to a room were locked in at night, stripped of their clothing and their dignity.

Escape and capture meant a whipping. James Clemens was one boy given this lesson on at least four occasions in 1870.[5] What became of James is anyone's guess. History did not record his fate.

Magill moved on from its early beginnings. Wineries were scattered at intervals across the foothills and the teeming rows of vines clutched and held the landscape in a sinuous and possessive grasp. But the wispy vapour of time steals quietly, devouring the present as it shapes a future from the past, sometimes in a whisper, sometimes in a roar.

In one violent symbolic thrust, on a March day in 1935, the future despatched the past, foreshadowing the deluge of motorised vehicles that was to come. Patrick Ryan and his sister Johanna left St Joseph's church in their horse-drawn fringed buggy that had been hand-crafted by Patrick and his brother Malachy. As Patrick turned the horse to cross Magill Road, the steel and glass hulk of a rarely seen motor vehicle slammed into them, killing Johanna and the horse and injuring Patrick.

Explosives tore open the face of the hillsides above the vines, exposing bare rock to be quarried. This set in motion processions of heavy vehicles on a continuous cycle of load and deliver, load and deliver, creating corridors of clamour en route. Layers of bitumen were poured to accommodate the growling beasts, as progress enforced its relentless will. Wineries were bought and sold and winemaking methods changed with the interplay of ownership. Locale was lost. The Grange vineyard diminished in its capacity to meet demand as the sole source of fruit for Penfolds world famous Grange Hermitage.

Eighty acres of vines were ploughed under overnight and the garden on the hillsides became a building site. Houses with fluted columns and ornamental balconies began to appear, like tiers on a wedding cake.

And all around the hills looked on in silence.

5

The times

It is a time of communication by device. The challenges of face-to-face human interaction can now be dodged—eyes and hands, clothes and hair, odours and itches, shrugs and twitches—all removed from the delivery of meaning in the message. Text messages and emails are void of the physicality of face-to-face human communication. Word for word the message is conveyed, and all that is required of the receiver is to gauge the mood, attitude, inference, connotation, context and intent of the sender, before making a reply.

Simple, isn't it?

It is a time that almost moves too fast for history. What counts as significant one day is not as significant the next. We hear about events the instant they occur and then they vanish in a vapour of memory. History chronicles human achievements, great and small. But recorded history still relies on who is telling the story.

How is it decided what a great or small achievement is? Becoming Australia's first female Prime Minister is great, but the clandestine way in which it happened renders it small. The Nobel Prize for Peace, presented to the first black president of the United States, is great. But bombs dropped on Yemen by US war planes killing 63 civilians, 23 of them children, while the ceremony took place, is far from great and yet is too horrific to be small. Some achievements lift the human spirit; others are a veneer to maintain the notion.

Magill was built on achievements, great and small.

From what Magill was to what it has now become will only be seen by those who care to look. The past is obdurate and is not easily changed. Looking through an opaque window, the other Magill becomes a photographic fusion of then and now. Images from an old book, splotched in cuttlefish-sepia hues wash and meld with the colours of the day. The other Magill is immanent in the buildings and in the layers of time crammed below life on the surface: below the streets and the traffic and the buildings, ingrained in rock and soil and memory, a place just around the corner in the imagination.

The frenzied traffic cauldron of Magill, Penfold and St Bernard's Roads becomes a dust bowl of bullock wagons loaded with timber from the stringy bark forests on the hillsides. The jutting hipbones of the plodding beasts sway rhythmically to the echoing crack of the teamster's long whip. Harnesses jingle and children squeal as they hitch a ride on a massive tree branch being dragged behind a dray to stop it barrelling out of control on the downhill run.

On the corner a shopkeeper cleans his window. Percy Sutton peers through the face-sized bubble in the grime. He likes keeping his butcher shop immaculate. His window displays are always enticing and he likes his customers to see what they are buying. He dips the wet rag into the bucket, squeezes out the excess and makes a wide sweep over the glass. Percy has witnessed many changes in the village: horse-drawn trams now roll by where once there were only mail coaches and bullock wagons. Now is a time when transport is worth more than land; when a pair of wagon wheels buys ten acres of land and both man and beast wear yokes. Fruit and vegetable growers transport their wares to market on foot, carrying baskets across their shoulders. The village is the halfway point on their journey to the city. Percy always notices a vigorous change of pace as they pass his shop and the World's End Inn comes into view. There they enjoy a drink or two and listen to tales of smugglers and dirty deeds. Then sleep in a soft bed before striking out again in the cool of early morning.

I step aside to let a grower from the hills pass by. He has four miles to walk before he reaches the city markets.

Freestone buildings still stand as evidence of the solid footings of Magill: the Institute, the Tower Hotel and the schoolhouse; foundations of place that have brought Magill from a robust past to an elusive present. They sit amidst modern buildings that do not quite fit—a rag-tag assortment of bland designs and simulacra: the history of Australian architecture spread along a few hundred metres of roadway. The Community Institute is closed. A Gothic-style window next to the doorway clashes with the graffiti-stained, half-moon glass panel above. The building is imprisoned in tall cyclone fencing: caged in case it escapes into the past before a profit can be made from it in the present. Weeds sprout from cracks in the tarmac around its foundations and from air vents in its walls.

Still it stands and waits.

On the corner of Pepper Street the old schoolhouse is overrun by gigantic ants, spiders and lizards that have emerged from some primeval cavern to drag it back through time. Opened in 1880 the schoolhouse fuses the past to the present. Today it is a modern art gallery but the building maintains its origins in the history of Magill. Across Pepper Street a modern post office seals the tomb of the World's End Inn: a smugglers' snug, lost with the boyhood dreams and stories of old men long gone. Nearby, a two-storey structure built by an undertaker and his son during a particularly slow season in 1903 remains a tenacious testament to diversity. The undertaker made sure his dabble in construction would outlast him. He used steel plates rendered with plaster for the walls—unique for its time. In stark contrast, the contemporary building opposite is made from pre-formed concrete slabs, a design that resonates with mid-twentieth century European Eastern bloc.

A crowd gathers on the footpath beneath the branches of a 'Strickland Eye,' one of the black gum trees that line the busy street. Cameras and mobile phones flash. Geometric slices of light illuminate the unctuous oxblood-coloured sap that oozes from the tessellated bark. A comatose koala is slumped like a lifeless doll in the fork of the tree. The koala's presence, so far from its habitat in the hills, is one of many wildlife sightings that have become a thrilling yet disturbing local phenomenon.

Behind the crowd is a real estate office that was once the police station. The cell block can still be seen, if you care to look, but who has the time.

I walk to the corner as a gust of wind whips the loose skirt of a young woman up around her waist. Her ear lobes glow in the glimmer of the red light that has just stopped a bus. Tired faces stare at her through the windows. She squeals a predictable 'Oh my God!' and giggles with embarrassment. The driver's eyes find mine through dirty glass; she looks oddly familiar.

It seems an impossible task to coax this elongated mass of glass and steel round the tight corner without scraping the light poles or colliding with cars from the opposite direction. But the driver rotates her torso in sync with her shoulders and arms, executing a graceful pirouette with the large steering wheel. She guides the beast to where it should go—around the corner with confident ease and concertinaed amidships—on both bus and driver.

I also turn the corner, but with somewhat less grace. I take my life in my hands and cross Magill Road just as a forward-scout paramedic plunges his station wagon, sirens wailing, into the intersection, causing more chaos and panic than the emergency he is going to.

6

The pacers

I fall in behind a brisk group of 'pacers' on Penfold Road. *Outpace me? Well, we'll just see about that.* They are heading uphill towards The Parade. These groups pound the pavements every day; their relentless footsteps seek a pathway from the ills that come with age. I count pepper trees, look up at a cloudless sky and pretend to be as nonchalant as my breathing will allow.

Ahead the traffic is at a standstill. A man is trying to coax a koala off the white line in the middle of Penfold Road. Schoolchildren watch happily until the man puts his hands on the animal's back in an effort to get it moving. The 'cute' creature bares its claws at the contact before bouncing its fluffy ears over to the footpath. It follows two children who now realise the koala is a 'wild' cute animal, and they increase their pace. The koala peels off and trots up Romalo Avenue towards the hills and home.

The place is rich with wildlife.

In the air the powerful form of a wattle bird, with its distinctive red jowls, swoops by in an aerobatic display: past windows, underneath pergolas and over endless lines of fences, traversing the long-familiar habitations of suburbia in search of insects. Noisy miners[8] screech and shriek then drone a throaty gargle when the dark presence of crows or magpies looms. These feisty little birds, with pirate-like yellow rings around their eyes, pull their necks deep into their plumage, lower their heads and prepare to attack their oversized foes. A sulphur-crested white cockatoo squawks a raucous greeting to all below, and above the hills a kestrel glides on thermals in the distant, vaporous blue haze. Delicate silvereyes and honeyeaters scoot urgently in and out of a holly tree and the melodic warble of the orange-beaked blackbird calls for a mate to come and admire his nest-building skills. Wood pigeons don't seem to need the admiration. They invite the female to a dilapidated nest of weeds and bits of plastic, soft-drink straws and bottle caps then proudly proclaim 'Look what I built for you: now let's mate!'

At the roundabout, two spectacular pines with immense trunks and evergreen foliage mushroom into the sky above the road. Every year flocks of yellow-tailed black cockatoos forage in the trees for cones laden with monkey nuts. Their glossy-black heads dip in and out of the green as they gauge the flow of traffic below. Down the cones fall: off roofs and bonnets and boots, and onto the tarmac in front of the oncoming flotilla. As the traffic slows, heavy tyres squash the cones, dislodging the nuts. When a raucous 'all clear' is given the cockatoos drop from the trees to shimmy their yellow tails out onto the road for the gathering.

On the ground families of koalas are making their way down from the hills to the main road, oblivious to traffic and noise. A mother koala with a baby on her back causes mayhem as she walks atop a brush fence in peak-hour traffic. Screeching tyres and drivers' angry voices do not deter her; nor do the hordes with camera phones that jump like paratroopers from moving cars to take pictures.

At dusk a boy climbs a tree in his yard to hand feed koalas their favourite eucalypt leaves.

As darkness falls, the 'gorilla' grunting of male koalas and the eerily human squeals of female koalas invade dreams and transport the night to the Serengeti. Hungry foxes haunt driveways and verandahs in search of food, and set the dogs a'barking all across the neighbour-hood. The wildlife visits have increased and we know why: development encroaches on habitat, restricting mating opportunities and food sources.

The pacers have now crossed Penfold Road and are heading west down The Parade. I try to keep up. *Just a little further and I'll turn back.* But my competitive streak will not let me stop, so I adjust my gait to theirs. These men are older than me, probably retirees—grey devils who claim ownership of footpaths, parks and cafés just because they can. They look happy and vibrant. *What the hell is wrong with them? They're not supposed to be happy and vibrant.*

Infinitely long legs lope past me. They are attached to the sweaty curves of a beautifully tanned body wearing Lycra shorts, tightly, and a Running Bare top, loosely, and … yes, it's a girl. I stumble as she glides by. She smiles warmly, displaying her spectacular white teeth to the pacers ahead of me—*bastards!*

I collapse onto a low brick wall outside a dental surgery. *Maybe I should have my teeth whitened.* I notice the pacers increase their speed to keep abreast of the young woman. They disappear into Kensington Park. I smack my envious lips at the taste of the delicious coffee they will soon be drinking at Taylor Blend[9] over on Hallett Road. The pacers are the healthy ones, the lucky few of their generation who can still clutch life close and will not let go.

I am wet and I smell. I look next door. A group of men and boys are gathered in front of a barbershop: George the Stylist: *maybe white teeth and a haircut.*

I promise myself the haircut and head back towards the hills and home.

7

the stylist

A burst of sunshine across a marbled sky makes me want to walk.

I arrive at the shop at twenty-to-ten, surprised to be the only one there. On the window candy-striped barber poles frame an enormous pair of yellow scissors and an equally large yellow comb. *George the Stylist* is written above them in flowing longhand. I press my nose to the narrow strip of glass between a venetian blind and the door jamb and peer into the gap, but the gloom inside gives nothing away. A whisper from behind startles me. I turn to face the bent and withered frame of an elderly man who points a knobbly finger at a notice inside the glass

Hours of business:
Monday to Friday 10am–6pm
Saturday 9am–12noon

Today is Saturday.

The old man gurgles. 'He's always late.'

The door is locked, the blinds are down and we are the only two in sight. Ten o'clock comes and goes and still I am staring at the lone butcher shop across the road. The elderly man sticks close to me to seal his place in a queue that is yet to form. At ten-past-ten, another elderly man arrives. He nods and offers a weak smile in our direction, unable to hide his disappointment at not being first in line. By quarter-past-ten the group, in front of this barber-less shop, consists of five men and two boys, who lean, sit, stand, shuffle, pace, smoke, and toe poke the concrete.

A faded, green early-model Holden stops across the street amid snickers of recognition and shreds of comments from the group, 'It's him,' 'He's here,' 'It's about bloody time.' A dark-haired man with a beard gets out of the car and crosses the road. As he gets closer the group becomes more animated and talkative and I hear a voice say, with grave concern, 'What happened to your face? Did you lose a tooth or something?'

The man doesn't answer. He keeps his head down and his hairy chin tucked into the cup of his shoulder-blade, like a boxer. I can see his cheek is swollen. The group fall silent, and step aside to allow him through. He climbs the steps to the porch and unlocks the door. Turning slowly, he looks down at the hushed gathering and without warning slaps his swollen cheek, deflating the swelling in a noisy burst of air and spit commonly known as a 'raspberry'.

'Just joking, boys, come in, come in and take a seat.'

The pantomime works. His lateness is forgotten as we all clamber in behind him into the Pied Piper's lair: sheep to be shorn. He snaps a switch and neon light flickers over images waiting in the shadows.

Humphrey Bogart scowls down from one wall. He is standing in blue mist at an airport in Casablanca. A Hawker De Havilland is propped with its nose to the sky on the runway behind him. Bogie is wearing his sack-tied-in-the-middle trench coat, belt knotted at the waist and buckle dangling. The coat is all folds and wrinkles, just like Bogie's face. And just like Bogie, the print itself seems to be struggling to stay inside its aged and worn frame.

Two bulky, but inviting, leather-look couches face one another. And, at the other end of the room, two impressive barber chairs are just as inviting. In front of the chairs large mirrors reflect the surroundings and give a full view of the room from every angle. I move awkwardly towards the first chair as the others squeeze onto the couches behind me.

'Not that one mate; it will fall apart,' someone warns me.

Another voice quips, 'He only uses the one near the kitchen, so he can get to his smokes.'

I tentatively move to the second chair and sit. On the bench top tools of the trade are lined up: four combs, two plastic and two steel, two pairs of scissors, a straight razor, electric clippers, a spray bottle, two small wooden-handled brushes, and not a jar of sculpting gel in sight.

'My name's Louie', says the face in the mirror.

He sweeps a cloak around me like a toreador. It has scents of talc and aftershave and memories of many other haircuts and other times.

'Is this your first time here?'

'Yes … I thought you were George… the sign on the window…'

'False advertising!' yells someone from the couch. 'His name's Louie not George, and as for stylist, what bloody stylist? Everybody leaves here with the same haircut!'

I scan the room. Louie is laughing as he prepares to cut my hair. He doesn't ask what I want done, and the anonymous voice behind me isn't about to let him.

'Hey, Louie, does your wrist get sore with all that cutting?' said the voice. 'Especially after what you get up to every night, shouldn't you be wearing glasses?' Laughter tumbles around the room. I watch Louie. He is enjoying this. The jibes are partly for my benefit, to introduce the new boy to the ways of the tribe.

'Shaadup, Nick, will ya?' said Louie.

The voice now has a name. Another scan and I can tell who Nick is from the expression on his face. We meet in the mirror. He wears a cheeky grin and a baseball cap which gives him an instantly likeable look. He is about average height, with dark eyes that flash with trouble. The wry humour, dark complexion and his name make me guess he's Greek.

'Don't pay him any attention; it only makes him worse,' said Louie.

'Why don't you play the man some decent music instead of all that old crap?' Nick persists.

'You wouldn't know decent music if it bit you on the ass,' says Louie. 'Hendrix, Led Zeppelin, Bob Dylan, Smoke on the Water ... we're talking *real* music, the greats, not the pop porn you watch every day.'

Nick is ready. 'Did you say popcorn? Because if you want to talk about corn then the stuff *you* listen to is what we should be talking about. Besides, I wasn't even born when most of those guys were killing themselves on sex, drugs and the corny music they play.'

Others join in, supporting Louie in a team effort against Nick. Outnumbered, he changes the subject.

'Are you going to take all day? I'm getting hungry.'

One of the young boys suggests he goes and gets some fish and chips.

'I don't eat fish and chips anymore,' says Nick, still annoyed at being howled down by the group. 'It's not the same since the Greeks stopped making them. These days it's fish and chips Asian-style, 'You want fried rice with that?' or 'How many dim sim or spring roll you want?' That's not real fish and chips; I want Greek fish and chips.'

Having successfully regained some status, Nick is now content to sit back and let someone else take over. But it doesn't happen. The two young boys share a magazine and I sense Louie has one eye on what they are reading.

The elderly man who is next in line watches Louie intently. He is either mesmerised by the swift movements of the scissors through my hair or he is using his mind, willing Louie to hurry up. Another man dozes on the couch and I begin to relax as Louie holds court. I study him in the mirror. He is in his late thirties or early forties, thinning on top with dark good looks set off by a wiry, dusty grey-black beard. I feel at ease relating to his reflection. The others seem just as comfortable. He knows so much about each of them. He talks about their families, their jobs, their women, football, racing, fishing, and he wants to know all about their lives since they last met. His eyes scrunch up and he jiggles with infectious laughter.

They crave his attention and he gives it to every one of them. How can he know them so well? Is a reflection easier to relate to than the real person? He listens, laughs, banters and argues with those in the room and those who have just arrived; all this without a hiccup in my haircut. He is the catalyst. The one who creates the environment everyone becomes a part of as they step through the door. It doesn't matter how you look or where you come from. The cost of entry is the common interests of men and respect for those around you.

Louie spins the chair, one way then the other, smiling and brushing hair from my face and his. Satisfied, he sweeps the cloak from my shoulders in one fluid motion, scattering hair across the floor. I stand and look at Louie. Marilyn Monroe smiles down approvingly from a leggy, full-size portrait above his head. I think she likes my haircut.

The cash register is broken. I hand Louie the money and he throws it into the open drawer.

'It hasn't worked in twenty years.'

8

No-man's land

Several weeks pass before I go back for another haircut.

Nick and Louie are talking at the far end of the room. The place is packed and all seats taken. Nick looks up as I step inside.

'You got an appointment?'

I am caught in no-man's land with the door at my back and certain humiliation ahead. Everybody stops talking to look at me. I give a wide grin, trying to project the persona of the true insider, but they know better. I clutch my book and bumble in circles, looking for a place to hide, when a wiry, fit-looking older gentleman speaks in a kind and soothing voice.

'Here … here mate; there's one seat left in the corner … only we don't have a dunces' hat, sorry.' He laughs and the room erupts with rowdy laughter.

Thanks for the welcome, you old bastard.

Silence ensues. I feel naked. The only sound is the click of Louie's scissors to *Bad Moon Rising* on the radio. I squeeze past assorted limbs and looks, newspapers and books, and make a lunge for the corner, hurdling two fat sofas on the way. Silence soars as I sink slowly into deep vinyl, causing squeaks and freeps and noises you can't imitate.

I overplay the detachment act: ignore the stares, open my book, and flick the pages in search of a fictitious page number.

'Have a look, the place is packed,' says Louie. 'It's like a doctors' surgery in here … we can cut your hair and take out your appendix while we're at it! Hey Nick, can you cut hair?'

'I'll give it a go; can't be any worse than you—you want me to put the 'CLOSED' sign up?'

I am no longer a curiosity.

There will be no cheating. The time-honoured sacred order of position in the queue will be strictly adhered to, so the older gentleman, whose name, I now know, is Barry, is summoned to the chair by the vigilant voices of authority.

The talk turns to football and it is a call-to-arms. Verbal Ping-Pong ricochets around the room then settles when the name of the famous Australian Rules football coach, Graham Cornes, is dropped by Barry.

'Yep, know him well. He's one of the good ones, not a bighead like some. I asked his help for a good cause once and he said no worries, happy to do it. Other lesser lights would say, 'How much will you pay me?' I interviewed him on 5RPH.'

'Oh, that station nobody listens to?' quips Louie, as Barry's head sinks into a mist of spray.

'We're rated above the ABC, so revise your F#*#ing estimate,' snaps Barry.

Louie goads him. 'But where do you find 5RPH on the radio dial?'

Barry doesn't bite.

'I listen to 5RPH all the time,' says a young man from the couch.

Louie changes tack.

'Cornsey's blood is with the Crows[10] but his sons play for Port Adelaide. What is that all about? How can one man be in two skins?'

Barry ignores him, but Nick chips in.

'Jesus, Louie, you got celebrities coming here!'

'This man has written stacks of books, been on radio, TV, every-thing. Barry, what's the most dangerous animal you've ever hunted?' asks Louie.

'Bush buck, it will attack you even when it's wounded. But I knew a bloke who killed a leopard with a small Remington.'

'Are you telling me, you knew someone who killed a full-grown leopard with a Remington shaver?'

'Bloody idiot! Only a barber would say that. It was a .22 Remington rifle.'

'He must have been crazy to go after a leopard with just a .22; was he mad?'

Barry lifts his head and surveys the room to make sure everyone is listening.

'He lost a leg in the First World War and I remember him saying that if the leopard attacks I'll offer my tin leg, it will take one bite and say, "Shit, what was that?"'

The laughter in the room stops abruptly when a woman comes to the front door. She walks inside and I expect an alarm to go off; some-thing like a submarine in dive mode. She has brought her elderly father for the first time and wants to make sure he is safely settled. The elderly man has a walking cane and is moving a little gingerly. Without a word, a young boy stands and offers his seat to the older man. Respect is important in Louie's place.

The man thanks the boy, takes the seat and crosses his hands over the bird figurine on the stock of his cane. He sits straight-backed, tanned and proud, and has a southern European look. His daughter asks what time she can pick him up. Louie smiles and tells her to come back in an hour or so. Nick coughs.

The elderly man stares at Louie for a few moments then says.

'You're a Langanis aren't you?'

Louie is taken aback, a little shocked. He stops cutting to look at the older man. His voice has an edge.

'You have me at a disadvantage…you seem to know me but I know nothing about you.'

The older man replies. 'What happens when two Greeks meet?'

Louie shrugs. We wait.

'They argue!' More laughter. Everyone is relieved.

'Savas… my name is Savas. I am eighty-three years old and I came to this country when I was *one*. I am the earliest migrant still alive in the state, if not the whole country, and I know all the Greeks who live here.'

'Where do you live?' asked Louie.

'I live near here, with my daughter and her family, but when I first came to this country my family settled in Port Pirie[11] with many other Greeks.'

'Port Pirie… did you know Con Polites?'

'Yes… yes… he was my best friend.'

The old man holds us in his hands with an epic story of struggle, hard work and success. We listen as he gives insight to a time and a life that cannot be found in history books. He is enjoying himself. An hour passes and his daughter comes and goes. Another hour passes and Louie is forced to introduce legislation to allow Mr Savas to advance in the queue. The daughter arrives for the third time just as Louie finishes brushing him down. Mr Savas leaves a happy man; making a promise to come back.

Louie thanks him and tells the daughter that if she ever needs to go shopping she is welcome to leave her father with him; with a promise not to corrupt him too much. Nick coughs.

I look at the faces of the men and boys. This is not just about getting a haircut. Their reasons go much deeper: it is a male domain. The shop has always been like this; it has history. Memories of a first haircut and the taste of a solid block of Black Cat chews given to a small boy by a barber named George still linger in the memory and the mouth of that small boy 35 years on. Fathers and sons grasp a rare moment of each other's time. It is a place to relate and share common interests, rich with stories that will never be lost. For all ages, nation-alities and occupations it is a refuge from a world that seems to be spinning faster on its axis. It is a place to hide from that world for a while, to catch your breath and wind down in the company of men.

9

The history lesson

The wait has been long. But now there are only three 'heads' left to cut. Two young boys have just gone and Louie is working on one head in the chair while engaging another on the couch — in a conversation I have no interest in whatsoever.

'They don't need us for sex any more. A friend of mine has a porn shop and she was telling me about a dildo with seven gears ... seven gears ... what do they need us for?'

The man on the couch shrugs. 'I've given up caring, Louie. I get all I want out of sex in three seconds and then I cuddle myself to sleep.'

Louie lifts the cut-throat razor from the neck of the man in the chair so he can laugh without drawing blood. I continue reading a newspaper that is now jiggling in front of my face.

Louie has more.

'She also told me she could sell Viagra every day of the week and twice on Sundays ... and it's not to the old blokes ... it's the young guys who take all the party drugs.'

The man in the chair stands up, clears his throat and smiles awkwardly for the first time during the exchange. Louie brushes him down, and then the man on the couch takes his turn in the chair.

'Sounds Spanish ... doesn't it?' he says, once settled.

Louie sprays a large cloud around the man's head and then enters the mist with a confused look. 'What does?'

'Viagra, Viagra sounds Spanish. I could have used plenty of it when I was over there ... the women, aw ... mate.'

'So you ran with the bulls?' Louie laughs, pleased with his analogy. 'Spanish women are either really, really beautiful or they are really, really ugly.'

The customer is having none of this: it's his story and he's not going to let Louie take it from him. 'I find it's the same with Greek women,' he says. 'They are either really, really beautiful or you have to shave them.'

The laughter leaves Louie's dark Greek eyes. He ponders before offering a reply that Plato would have been proud of: 'There is beauty wherever you go in the world.'

'Yeah ... yeah ... you're right, Louie,' the man stammers, trying desperately to redeem the situation. 'It's just that I feel sorry for some women who have to live with ethnic traits that can spoil their looks.'

Louie voice is flat. 'You sure you want a number one comb? Number one's pretty short.'

'Yeah ... yeah ... do it, mate,' comes a nervous reply.

The number one comb does the job. Louie ruffles the loose hair from the soft spikes on the shaven skull with his hand, just for luck. The two men part with smiles, shoulder slaps and a handshake. I step up to the chair.

Louie reaches around the door jamb to the kitchen for his smokes; lights one up, takes a deep draw, and blows a long, white, swirling tail through the doorway. The tail ends in a series of elongated smoke-rings as Louie imitates the gulps of a goldfish.

'You're not in a hurry are you?' He asks.

We laugh at the absurdity of the question, our tiredness making it funnier. It has been a marathon day, and I am ready to sleep as he begins to cut. I listen to the click of the shears and watch a tuft of hair land on the footrest far below. My head bobs at the faded inscription between my splayed feet: Barbers' Supply Co., St Louis USA.

'You heard of Max Schubert?' Louie's voice buzzes in my head.

'Waa...yep ... yep ...' I dribble. 'He created Penfolds Grange Hermitage.'

'Max used to fall asleep when George cut his hair,' says Louie.

I'm not surprised, if he had to wait as long as I did.

'Do you drink Grange?'

I explain that Grange is beyond my means, and the closest I ever get to it is to gaze longingly at where it's made, close to my house on Penfold Road. Louie knows the house well. He proceeds to give me a history lesson about former owners who still come to him for a haircut.

'Yeah, Louie ... I ... I'm ...'

He keeps going. The original owner was Hurtle Walker. His son, Norm Walker, was a famous winemaker like his dad and a champion ex-footballer for the local, Norwood football club—the Redlegs. Norm is great mates with Max Cooper of Cooper's Brewery. Norm's son Nick is also a winemaker. He owns a winery called O'Leary Walker at Watervale up in the Clare Valley north of Adelaide. Nick also played for the famous Redlegs. Louie grabs a breath. I jump in.

'I know, Louie. I'm writing a book about them.'

He gives me a *look* followed by a succinct, but smiling, 'Bullshit.'

10

The beautiful book

Louie delicately removes a blade from the cut-throat razor and inserts a new one. This cut-throat razor looks real, but technology has caught up and replacing a new blade is easier than stroking a leather strop.

'It will be the beautiful book,' he proclaims.

'Now you're putting the pressure on.'

'Got room in there for George?'

'Tell me about him.'

George the Stylist could cut hair, engage in conversation and listen to the races at the same time. It didn't matter if he was winning or losing or how much money was going round the track with the horses: he never flinched at the result nor left you with a haircut full of holes. And George always had sweets in the shop, to help young boys get over the trauma of that first haircut.

Anybody who was anybody came to George's shop. He could hold a conversation with any of them: brain surgeon or bartender, MP or mechanic, football player or cricketer. It didn't matter who you were or what you did. It is the same today.

Anyone who comes to Louie's shop seems to know everyone else, or know someone who knows someone else. It is like being a couple of handshakes away from knowing the whole of Adelaide. When you look around you realise its more than a barber shop; it's a cultural gallery where the artefacts are brought by those who gather there.

In one corner of the shop, in an old display cabinet, you will find a pod of cigarette lighters. They sit amid a clutter of collectables: bottles of wine, sports memorabilia, sports almanacs, timeworn photographs and ancient engine-oil bottles—Shell, BP, Amoco and Caltex. In the centre, a tarnished, burnt-orange lighter rests on a translucent, hand-carved alabaster block. Another lighter is a delicately honed Grecian urn. A peacock's tail, inlaid in its side, is fanned in colourful display. Alongside, stands a slender, stylish gold lighter on a yellowish-green jade base. The lighter looks silky smooth to the touch, begging to be picked up. One lighter stands out from the rest. It is a biplane made of burnished brass, a miniature of *The Spirit of St Louis.*

Louie mentions a current collecting fetish and personal items, previously relegated to attics and sheds and dark corners in cupboards begin to appear. Treasured offerings to share and talk about that would otherwise be lost: each a cultural artefact, each a building block in the character of this pocket of culture.

I sit and watch small shredded clumps of my hair slide down the glassy surface of the cape and slip silently over my knees to tumble gently to the floor.

Louie learned much about life and people from George the Stylist. George died on the ninth of May 2000, but his legacy lives on through his friend, Louie: another kind of stylist.

I doze and muse and listen to the rasp of the razor on my neck. *The beautiful book eh? How did it all begin?*

11

We need an audience

A bodiless, panic-stricken, frazzled head gapes at us from around the office door. She looks at my colleague and pleads 'We need an audience, Mia.'

Publishers of a local wine magazine have set up an information session at the university to give third-year writing students the opportunity to enter a competition offering a cadetship and a trip to the London Wine Show. But only an embarrassingly small number of students have shown up.

Now cadetship implies youth. But the romantic notion of working in wine and a trip to London is irresistible, so I suck up the drooping middle-fat, hoist the jowls, force my face into a taut, wrinkle-free mask and wobble my way to the meeting room.

A well-dressed young man stands at the front of the room talking casually to his audience. Student numbers have now swollen to five. He looks up as we enter. The look tells me he knows we are there just to fatten the room. But I have other ideas.

Our host begins. 'The rules of the competition are simple: interview a local wine personality for a feature in the magazine and pass a sensory test ...'

I stop listening and let my mind wander ...

∞

The house I live in was built in 1924 by Hurtle Walker, a famous winemaker.

If only it were possible to interview him.

On moving into the house, imagination overtook curiosity. I was intrigued by old photographs and even older documents and wine labels I found. I developed the annoying habit of attaching a story to every new discovery and burdening anyone who would listen. Weekend gardening became archaeological digs. Artefacts I uncovered held no significance or mystery to anyone other than me: old wine bottles, a corroded medallion from a wine show, champagne corks with those squiggly wire things still wrapped around them. They all had to have a story. I was even convinced I had found a cannonball (not a shot-putt) in a garden in suburban Magill, far and away from any war or any known historical locations of gun emplacements.

One photograph of the house, *circa* 1932, shows a woman sitting on the front porch wall looking pensively out over a dusty Penfold Road. I traversed and quizzed every millimetre of that photo on a computer screen.

The frontage looks wider. Have the neighbours encroached on my land over the years? Is that a chicken coop?

The vines stretch across the hills behind the house and there are few dwellings to be seen. As I navigate the space in front of the porch, the eye of technology reveals a previously unnoticed image of a small child sitting on a tricycle. Who is the woman? Who is the child? Was the winemaker who built the house standing on Penfold Road taking the picture?

Before long the house began to generate stories that craved to be written.

The sun's rays left the horizon, filtering a pathway through the foliage of many trees before being parsed and separated by the plum tree in front of the old house. The rays of scattered light struck a window, spilling into a room, and were captured by a keyhole. Out through the keyhole and onto a wall at the dark end of a passage, they projected a filigreed image of a woman sitting on a chair under the plum tree in the garden. Delicately dressed she sat, all lace and ruffles beneath a wide brimmed sun hat, reading her book, oblivious that time had passed (Neill 2008).

'For God's sake what is it this time?'
'I don't know … it … came … through the keyhole,' I whispered.

Nervous excitement gripped me when the image first appeared on the wall. Ribbons of sunlight flickered and danced from the keyhole and probed the darkness of the hallway like a projector in an old cinema. I slid across the floor boards; silk-silent in sock soles so as not to disturb … whatever it was … and peeked into the garden. Was she *really* there? The slightest breath of movement changed everything. The veil of illuminated white blossoms that covered the plum tree parted and I could see there was nobody there. I squinted in the terra cotta glow of a late afternoon sky, to anchor a coordinate of the sun's position. The burning orb hung heavy in a space between the vast foliage of two distant gum trees. I looked at my watch. I had my anchor.

'Why are you whispering?'

The tiny circle of light unnerved her. She saw the image immediately. I pointed out the distinct delicate features, the sunbonnet and the book.

'I think the house … wants … my attention.'

'And you think this is an apparition?'

I twitched, mocking insanity.

She sighed and walked away.

The image left with the sun. But the following day I waited, and when the sun got to that place in the sky where the coordinates were set, the light-show began again and the image returned. This time I kept it to myself. Over the next few days, changes in the balance of conditions gradually elongated the tiny circle of light until it became a splash on the wall. I tried to recapture the image by being there earlier or later or by constantly changing the angle of the door. But how do you capture sunlight in a keyhole? The lady vanished.

My wanderings in and out of the hallway, mumbling to myself, began to disturb the balance of matrimonial harmony. But the need would not leave me. Hurtle Walker was long gone. I could not talk to him. I could only muse about what he might say:

'When did it happen?'

Not long after we moved into the house.

'And you think it was an apparition?'

I think I wanted it to be.

'It's just a story.'

But it did happen. It's all in the telling. I wrote stories about you too.

'What kind of stories?'

About your childhood

'But you weren't there.'

No, I wasn't, that's the problem. No-one alive was there.

'So you made them up.'

Well, yes and no. They exist in the gaps between the living and the telling.

'And what did you come up with?'

You'll have to wait and see. I'm still working on them.

'I'll let you know if you go too far.'

I wouldn't have it any other way.

∞

A finger pokes me in the ribs; 'you're snoring.' I sit up and nod an apology to our host, who continues:

'Taste and identify two reds and two whites; answer a series of questions about the wines and winemaking in general to complete the sensory test.'

What? Tasting? And questions? God, I never could taste the flavours in wine that the aficionados go on about: pepper, chocolate, strawberries or gooseberries. I've never even eaten a gooseberry for that matter. They have got this all wrong. Some of the students don't look old enough to drink wine anyway.

'... A spittoon will be provided and you must be over eighteen to enter the competition ...'

Well I am over eighteen and technically still a student, but I have no use for a spittoon. I need a wine personality.

12

Ormond Avenue

The small child on the tricycle in the old photograph turned out to be the winemaker's son, Norman Walker, a famous winemaker like his father. As chance would have it, he lived so close that our houses were separated only by a narrow street. While both houses face busy Penfold Road, they flank one another in Ormond Avenue, where the to and fro and the everyday doings of the neighbourhood take place. In time I would come see the space between our houses as a social, cultural and historical thoroughfare.

Ormond Avenue is a short avenue. At its eastern end a tall pine grows from the middle of the road. Three trunks spring from its base and its roots are visible beneath the surface of the surrounding bitumen. To the left is Young Park, a shaded walk-through that connects to Romalo Avenue. And to the right La Perouse Avenue adjoins The Parade. Straight ahead, behind a high wire fence, the white walls and yellow shutters of gracious Romalo House catch the sunlight, in an arbour of native trees, wildflowers and unique native shrubbery.

Ormond Avenue is the staff of a trident thrust east: of streets, landmarks and people, in a slice of suburban Magill where voices waning in time wait to be heard.

13

The boys

Each Monday they park their cars in the avenue close to his house. The elderly male drivers stroll by carrying various beverages and what look like lunch boxes. They go quietly to the den in the garden. But on Thursday evenings they rumble and thunder and howl at the moon, followed by much riotous laughter and tribal chants that ring-out across the landscape. It is daylight so I feel safe.

I cross Ormond Avenue in search of Norman Walker.

The den is a wooden structure built on stilts close to the main house. Long windows set in brick-clad walls frame the doorway and an elevated foot-worn porch spans the front. In the garden pink and red camellias dress a patch of grass where a wrought iron table and two chairs sit and wait beneath the wide limbs of a tall tree. I sense movement through the window and climb the steps to the porch. Laughter booms from inside as I knock on the door.

'Is that you Coop? Why are you knocking the bloody door?'

The door swings open. The tall man I saw on the day of the auction, with the striking white hair, towers above me. It has to be him.

To say he is a tall man doesn't quite cover it. He looks down at me from the height of the open doorway with a stoop of necessity. He stands lanky and languid, unhurried and relaxed as he lowers his head to catch what I might have to say. His skin glows red under an enormous grin that connects the corners of his mouth to his cheekbones. Every fold traces easily the tracks where many smiles have gone before. Above the cheekbones blue eyes assess me out of scrunched up, fleshy eye sockets, and at the summit is the hair, the thick, white, curly hair that frames his head like a helmet.

'Norm Walker,' he beams. His paw engulfs my hand ... 'Come in, come in.'

I peer into the gloom and wait for my eyes to adjust. In front of me a three-quarter sized snooker table takes up most of the space. Behind the table pool cues lean at convenient angles against a cue rack where cubes of chalk sit deep in blue dust along the top. A kitchen sink with a small cupboard is in one corner of the room. To the right of the sink an open door reveals a shower and vanity unit. Above the pool table a scoring scroll is mounted next to a neat assortment of photographs on the wood-panelled wall.

In awkward silence I look to my right. Two men sit in a disarray of very low chairs giving the impression they are squatting on the floor. In front of them, playing cards, a cribbage board, and half-filled glasses of red wine share the space on a small card table. Their faces have the same glow as Norm Walker's, and they grin cheerfully in the dim light. On the wall above their heads hangs a large square board that appears to be an honour roll of some kind. And looking down over the honour roll is a perforated sad-looking weather vane, a Rooster full of holes.

Norm breaks the silence. 'This is the bombardier and the dentist.'

The who, and the what?

I reach down to shake their hands and resist the urge to pat them on the head.

'I live across ...' I began.

'You bought dad's old house,' says Norm. 'You paid too much for it.'

'Well ...' I stammer.

'Would you like a snort?'

'Sorry?'

'A snort ... a drop ... you know, a drink.'

The look on their faces told me I should not say no.

'Um ... yes please.'

'Grab a seat,' said the dentist, 'no not that one ... you'll go arse over head."

My knees grind and scream for relief as I lower myself into the chair. We are now three dwarfs waiting for Snow White. The two men look to be in their late 70s or early 80s. The dentist eyes me suspiciously, waiting for me to state my business. The furrows in his forehead deepen with my silence. The bombardier, on the other hand, is a pleasant-looking man with a suave manner and the rosiest cheeks I have ever seen. While the dentist is definitely Australian, the bombardier's look strikes me as English or Scottish.

At the far end of the room Norm is bent low over the small sink and appears to be giving a glass a quick lick 'n' spit at knee level. He shakes the drops onto the floor and pours red wine into the glass. Back to our small group, he hands me the wine then lowers his long limbs gracefully into what looks like a higher chair than the rest.

I raise the glass, say 'Cheers' and take a sip. It tastes *bloody awful.*

'Cleanskins,' says Norm.

'And to you too,' I grimace, hoisting the glass again.

'No, no ... the wine ... it comes in a bottle without a label so it's called a cleanskin.'

'Who makes it?'

'We don't know who makes it,' says bombardier.

I touch the glass to my lips.

'Wouldn't it be better if you knew who made it?'

I look at each of them. They are no longer smiling.

'But if you did...you would have to pay more for it,' says Norm.

'I know nothing about wine; that's why I'm here.'

They are smiling again.

I tell them about the competition: the interview and the sensory test. And confess that I don't know a cleanskin from a redskin. I enjoy wine but find it impossible to distinguish individual flavours in red or white wines. I babble on with hardly a pause for breath, and try to explain my fascination with the old house. I keep the lady in the garden story out of the conversation in case they decide I need another cleanskin. My monologue fades as I look at each of their faces and realise they are now smiling in a curious, numb-faced sort of way.

Are they drunk?

'Are you a Pom?'[12]

I look at the dentist. It's my accent. 'No, no ... I'm Irish.'

'Oh ... that explains a lot,' he winks.

They begin to talk rapidly, competing to be heard. I have started something. Cramped joints crack and pop as grunts of effort pull them out of the low seats. They limp and bounce and dip their way around the walls of memories, bending and stretching stiff appendages.

Norm points to a boy in an old photograph. The boy is surrounded by other young boys in knickerbockers and straw hats, and grim-faced men in drooping moustaches. There are no smiles in this photo except for one man standing at the rear. Baskets and buckets for picking dot the scene. And a wagon filled to the brim with grapes waits to be dragged away.

'That's my dad, Hurtle Walker; he was about twelve then,' Norm says proudly. They turn and look at me for a response. I mutter a weak ... 'Wow.'

We move to the large board below the weather cock. They point with their wine glasses and chorus in unison at columns of nicknames painted at the bottom of the board. They become boisterous in their excitement to be first to connect stories to names in a flurry of words and gestures. Their stories criss-cross the room, resonating in the space.

I arrange to return the next day to interview Norm, and bid farewell to the boys in the chairs, and the boys on the wall.

∞

The following evening there are two chairs set up on each side of the card table. A writing pad and two pens sit waiting to begin. Norm is scrubbed and polished with a crisp aura of aftershave about him. He is a man who cares about his appearance and is stylishly dressed. I am nervous.

'We'd better not have one until after the interview,' he says.
Oh God, he means a cleanskin.
'Good idea.'
'Where would you like to start?'
'How about the beginning,' I reply.

Silent seconds pass as he looks at the pictures on the wall. His eyes settle on the photograph of the boys in the vines.
'My father Hurtle Walker was born in Ellis Street, Magill in 1890. He was ten years old when he first picked grapes in a vineyard.'

14

Dynasty

I am staggered by the scope of what Norm Walker is telling me. Stories etched on his memory come in a flood of detail and emotion. The Walkers are not just local wine personalities; the Walkers are a winemaking dynasty: Hurtle, Norm, Nick, and Nick's son, Jack. Norm Walker's recollections are epic: the early years of a young industry, Hurtle Walker as a boy, heroism on the Somme, skilled artisans of fine wines, high esteem in the wine industry, the cornerstone of wine-making in Magill, life and family and connections to *place*. I will look at Magill through different eyes from now on.

We have spent a few hours together and I am warming to this man. He is not old in the way we stereotype older people. Our back-grounds are certainly different. But his easy, unpretentious manner relaxes me and I feel comfortable and welcome in his company. Humour suits him and his quips are original and quick. He doesn't complain or give a monologue on the current state of his health, and he is humble about his achievements, yet proud and lavish in his praise when it comes to his family.

The interview is over. *Do I have enough for an article? I have enough for a book.* I sit and scribble and watch him as his eyes dwell on the photo of the boys in the vines: his portal to the past.

Grape picking is backbreaking work with little pay: pick a ton a day or get on your way. There was little else for boys to do around Magill in 1900—no Play Station or Wii or Nintendo DS; no flat screen TV, and no McDonalds. Picking grapes during vintage meant they could miss school. But even though they were with their friends it couldn't have been much fun. The heat, the flies, the dead weight of baskets filled with grapes, and blisters on their hands from the clipping tool would have seen to that.

Norm still contemplates the photograph and I wonder if I should leave. Maybe looking back upsets him somehow.

'Look at the way those boys are dressed,' he says. 'Not much risk of skin cancer when you're covered up like that.'

I notice crusty lesions on his arms. In his day, when you played football, tennis or cricket, as he did, you were considered a sissy if you covered up. Of course, being caked in mud during the football season helped a bit. He looks tired. I've stayed too long.

'Norman …'

'Norm.'

'Norm?'

'Or Stalkie …'

'Stalkie … what's Stalkie?'

'It's my Early Marchers nickname.'

'Is it … Stalky as in bean-stalk, or Storky as in long-legged bird?'

'I'm not sure … or Lofty, or Stretch …'

How did we get into this?

'Okay … Stalk … Norm … What's an early marcher?'

The Early Marchers are a family of men whose names are inscribed on the honour roll of the Innamincka esky. The large board hanging on the wall is the enormous lid of that esky.[13]

Innamincka: where is this going?

15

Lords of Innamincka

On Innamincka Ice Box Mondays, the chemist, the diver, the stock-broker, the brewer and the pilot gather at the home of the winemaker to have lunch, drink a little wine and tell stories, as they have done for over 40 years. One by one they arrive, parking their cars in the quiet street while the rest of the neighbourhood gets on with the every-dayness of suburban life. They make their way to the winemaker's den in the garden behind the house, carrying their sandwiches and a bottle or two. Once inside, they become Medic, Burch, Hoppy, Rooster, Coop, and Stalkie, names on an honour roll mounted on the wall. The honour roll is the lid of what was an enormous icebox. The icebox is gone now — stolen by someone who kindly left the lid.

The Early Marchers, as they call themselves, began when a group of Apex members got to the club's mandatory retirement age of 40. It was a young man's club, Apex had said, and in the early 1970s forty was regarded by most as getting on. But for this group of ten it was just a beginning. They planned weekends away together at a beach property owned by one of the members. They fished from small aluminium boats called 'tinnies,' cast lines from the beach, dabbled for fish at night under spotlight and shot a few rabbits. And if you won a bed in the house, you were lucky; the rest slept outside on the lawn.

Their numbers grew, as did the list of nicknames: Winesy, Harry the Horse, Bosun, Desert Trek Dick, Pancho, Pom, Spanner, Scotty, Spot, and many more. And as the numbers grew so did the adventures and the derring-do. The weather vane on the roof of the beach house was despatched with a twelve-gauge shotgun because it pointed in the wrong direction for too long and that meant no fishing. The remains of the unfortunate cock now adorn the wall above the honour roll in Norm Walker's den. What had Apex unleashed?

The group quickly outgrew the beach house and decided it was time to look further afield. After much deliberation Innamincka[14] was chosen. Research had revealed that, although it was a very dry place, it had a pub and one could do a little sightseeing. Coop, the brewer, however, lodged a protest. He was not going that far away unless he could have six cold stubbies a day as he always did. There was no argument. But if he had to have six cold beers a day, then they all had to have six cold beers a day. Coop was given the task of designing an icebox with the capacity to suit their needs. And so the Innamincka Ice Box was born, a model of ingenuity and engineering excellence. It was years ahead of its time, a monstrous cavern of an esky, insulated by the latest technology in spray-on foam and cooled by block ice. It accommodated all their needs and some food as well. And it worked superbly. The beer froze solid and they couldn't drink it.

Coop supplied the beer because Coop made beer; Stalkie made wine so he pulled enough wine out of one of the vats up at the cellars. Spot chipped in 20 kilos of prawns from Venus Bay. And a whole sheep came fully dressed from a country property near Penola. They would live like lords: lords of Innamincka.

The name Early Marchers was chosen because trips were planned for early in March of each year. That way the women, who were not invited, would know what to expect and it gave the men something to look forward to.

Forty years on, in Norm's own words, 'that file has all but folded now; can't get enough together to go away. Most of the wives seem to have something wrong with their health so the husbands are sticking close to home.'

There are only eight Early Marchers left and they remain resolute. Those who are able still come to Norm's den in the garden to have lunch, play snooker and share memories.

The bombardier and the dentist are Early Marchers. Only the dentist's nickname is Medic and he is actually a chemist called Max. *It makes sense, in an Irish sort of way.* Max the medic provided the stoppers and the starters for Early Marcher bowel management, plus insect repellent, sunscreen and outlandish hangover potions. The bombardier was not a bombardier. He was a pilot who flew Lancaster bombers during World War Two and his name is Craig.

Each nickname holds a story.

Hoppy the diver hopped everywhere. He lost a leg to a train while dangling his feet over the station platform when he was a teenager. From then on he set out to prove he could do anything any other man could do. He became a high-board diver, walking to the end of the board on his hands to somersault over the edge into the water far below. He also became a sky diver and a deep sea diver. Hoppy the deep sea diver searched the ocean depths off the coast of Indonesia in a quest to recover the bell from the wreck of the Australian warship, HMAS *Perth*. After a fruitless search he learned the bell had already been taken by an Indonesian diver. Back onshore, Hoppy made his voice heard at the highest levels of the Indonesian government. He insisted the bell go to its rightful place, to the Australian War Memorial, Canberra.

Hoppy brought the bell home.

∞

'Norm ... the stories are great ... but I should get going.'

A warm, all-knowing smile fills his face. I feel bad. All he wants is some company. His eyes twinkle.

'We better have that snort then.'

Oh bugger ... Cleanskins.

I grab my notebook. *If it's a snort he wants, a snort he'll get.*

'Okay, Norm ... I'll drop this home ... be back soon.'

'I'm not going anywhere,' he says.

16

Night of the neophyte

I wander the racks, staring aimlessly at endless rows of black bottles. *Some wine cadet I'd make.* My expertise in choosing good wine is guided by the price tag: Church Block, Hill of Grace, St Henri and of course Grange. And I couldn't afford any of those. I've been here for a while and the bottle shop boy is getting suspicious. I spend less time in the library. I search for rows with only a few bottles: Cabernet Sauvignon, Shiraz, Merlot, and Pinot Noir. The wine must be good if the row beneath is almost empty, either that or it's cheap wine, or it's good wine going cheap, or the kid just didn't fill the rows when he should have. I read some labels. *Let's see, rich peppery ... full bodied ... chocolate aftertastes ... yeah right. What's this? Light reflects ... ruby red ... perfusion of soft aromas waft down the valley ... God! Shall I take the condiments or the painting in a bottle?*

I finally settle on a red called Scrubby Rise because I like the name. It reminds me of how I get up in the morning. The wine is a blend of grape varieties, one of which I cannot pronounce so it must be good.

∞

'What have you got there?' asks Norm.

I step into the den to see four bottles of wine and four glasses neatly arranged on a bright yellow vinyl sheet covering the pool table.

'It's a Wirra Wirra, Scrubby Rise ...'

He takes the bottle and studies it closely. 'They make good wine,' he says.

I lean on the pool table, grip the ring on the corner pocket and puff out my chest, happy that he thinks I have picked a good wine.

'What's all this?' I sweep my arm over the line-up of bottles and glasses. He walks to the far end of the room. The Scrubby Rise disappears and I never see it again. He reminds me about the sensory test for the competition and I know he is itching to demonstrate his knowledge.

'I never meant you to go to all this trouble, Norm.' But inside I am happy he did.

He picks up a knife with a long curved blade and attacks the neck of the nearest bottle. The bottle looks old. It screeches and squeaks as he skins it. Removing the cork is a problem. The very professional-looking high-tech cork remover contraption only manages to pull the cork out a little way before it begins to crumble.

'That had to happen,' he mutters, unfazed.

An ancient corkscrew with a worn and burnished wooden handle appears from nowhere. What remains of the cork squeals but finally yields to the inevitable. This wine did not want to leave the bottle. Norm slops some slush from the neck into the sink, to get rid of God knows what floating on top. He pours two glasses and puts the bottle back on the table. I read the label. Penfolds Coonawarra Cabernet Sauvignon-Kalimna Shiraz, vintage 1967. *Jesus, it's over 40 years old.* He opens a second bottle without a hitch. This time he pours what look like two urine samples. Tyrrell's aged release Semillon. *Fifteen years old.*

He asks me what I know about wine. I tell him I am a complete novice, a neophyte, and offer the feeble schoolboy joke about throwing a grape in the air that comes down plonk. Isn't that how wine is made? He smiles patiently.

I take a glass of the Semillon. Norm does the same. He holds his glass by the stem and swirls it around to release the flavours. I take the stem between my forefinger and thumb and swirl. My pinkie is extended and I have a strange urge to place my other hand on my hip. He holds his wine up to the light. I do the same.

'What do you see?'

'It's very yellow.'

'That's a good start. Now look at the meniscus.'

'What's that?'

He explains that you drink wine with your eyes before you put it to your lips. The meniscus is the ring around the top of the wine that shows the clarity of the colour. I peer into my crystal ball searching for enlightenment. A shimmering hoop of light, the colour of Van Gogh's tulips, encircles the golden liquid.

'A painting in a bottle,' I murmur.

'Eh?'

'Nothing...'

I continue to stare into the glass, fascinated. 'Oh ... yeah,' I drone, 'the meniscus.' I roll the word around my tongue savouring the sound and say it again slowly: 'men...is...cus.'

'At least we can try to make you look like an expert,' he smiles. 'Now, have a whiff.'

Norm dips his nose into the glass and takes a sniff. I put the glass up over my nose and simulate a vacuum cleaner. The wine goes north and I cough and gag uncontrollably. *Is this a snort?*

Through watery eyes I can see he is grinning. *I'm glad you're enjoying yourself.* I pinch my own stem with forefinger and thumb and wring the droplets of yellow liquid from my nostrils.

'What did you smell?'

'Not much, Norm ... I was choking at the time.'

'Try again, only not too far in.'

This time I bring my nose to the glass, not the glass to my nose, and allow the aromas to 'waft up the valley.'

'It smells like wine — what *should* it smell like?'

So the lesson begins. He trips a light fandango eloquently through the lyrical language of wine. It is almost poetic. I watch him closely. His face glows with pleasure. I feel honoured at his eagerness. He takes me into the vines in warm sunshine and ignites my imagination with his knowledge. He talks about wine aromas that mimic fruits like cherries, strawberries, peaches or melons: aromas that reveal where the grapes were grown and the minerals in the soil; the perfume of wildflowers and the flavours imparted by limestone and other stone. He explains that wine is a fusion of smells with taste. You don't actually taste a wet stone. It is aromas coupled with taste, with several senses reacting at the one time. Otherwise the taste of wine would only have a single dimension, like fruit juice or a soft drink. He speaks of the touch of wine, the soft or sharp feel of it in your mouth: light, medium or heavy in body, silky-smooth or chewy to taste. How the wine whispers to your senses: front tastes, back tastes and aftertastes, short palates, long palates, and no palates. And he describes the sensations on the tongue as taste buds engage nasal receptors to create a climactic sensory experience.

Wow!

Now that's not *exactly* how he said it, but it was how I heard it. The language, the ritual and the mystique build excruciating anticipation much the same as foreplay. I was never any good at foreplay so I gulp down the wine and conjure a response in my mind – *smooth, full and rich with a long palate*. I cannot wait to tell him. He sips from his glass, holds the wine in his mouth for a few seconds then swallows. 'It's been in the bottle too long,' he says. 'What do you think?'

'Well I … not bad, not bad, but you're right, it's probably been in the bottle too long.'

He reaches for another glass on the pool table. 'Let's try the red.'

We try more than one. And the more we try the less I can tell about them. But it is good wine, with not a cleanskin in sight. It is making me mellow. The sensory test is Friday. Two days away. I will never 'get' the fruit thing. Maybe I have my dad's taste buds; he was a Guinness man. I decide that if I cannot taste the fruit on Friday, I will just say I am Catholic and can only taste fish, or I will make it up. A strawberry is a strawberry anywhere in the world, but if they start with the gooseberries, I am walking out.

'Not everybody has a good palate,' Norm says, trying to reassure me. 'Max Schubert had a great palate.'

He tops up my glass.

'Who is Max Schubert?'

'Max created Penfolds Grange Hermitage.'

He tells me the story of a wine that yearned to be made and of the man who yearned to make it. So steadfast was Max Schubert in his need, he risked everything. Early developments were disappointing and he was told to 'let it go.' But nothing great comes easy. The hard way is the only way. He went to extraordinary lengths to finish what he started. Norm believed Max was a little sceptical of the science. He was uncomfortable in the company of oenologists. To Max wine-making was more organic than scientific, where intuition and an exceptional palate resulted in better wine.

In the early days the wine industry was like family. They helped each other out. If cork was in short supply, or if a Penfold's delivery of cork was sitting on a dock somewhere, Max would phone Norm at the Romalo cellars and Norm would send up a pallet of cork, and back down came a couple of bottles of the 'good stuff.'

'I had more Grange than you could poke a stick at,' says Norm.

I gulp more wine. He sips. I look at the wine in my glass and the Innamincka icebox lid on the wall. Two Maxes: Maxwell Cooper and Max Schubert. One creates a unique wine for wine lovers across the globe; the other builds an enormous esky and creates a bond between twenty men that lasts for over 40 years—

I am officially, philosophically merry.

"Max Schubert, Penfolds Grange and the *Lords of Innamincka*, eh ... Norm?"

My tongue is a tiny fish flapping around behind my teeth and I whine the name Innamincka down my nostrils as though I have a speech impediment. Norm the sipper sounds fine.

'Yes. Good wine and good mates; I've been pretty lucky. That esky worked well, too well. The bloody beer froze solid and we couldn't drink it.'

I suddenly think of 'Coopers Doopers'. The idea is brilliant. Coopers could freeze their magnificent pale ale in plastic tubes to have on a hot day, a kind of adult 'Super Dooper'. I am now at stage two—officially, idiotically merry. I laugh at my own internal wit, and it is infectious. Norm's face scrunches up as he joins my mood. It feels good to laugh with him and he is enjoying himself. But it's time to go: *trop de vin*. I drain my glass and make an effort towards the sink.

'Don't worry about that,' he says, 'you can do the washing-up next time.'

It's good to hear he expects me to come again.

'Just one more thing, Norm—did your son Nick make the cleanskin I had yesterday?'

He makes a noise akin to a grunt.

'No ... definitely not O'Leary Walker wine ... one of the boys brought that ... they don't like paying too much. Some of what they bring turns out to be plonk,' he grins.

17

Children of the corn

Terroir (ter'war)—a whole bloody semester of French and that word never came up. It probably has something to do with terror, like I feel now. If not terror then terra, as in terra firma ... I'll go with terra firma. The red is Cabernet Sauvignon or is it Shiraz? The white is definitely Riesling. Remember to pronounce Shiraz, Shira, without the 'z' as Norm does. That must be how the French pronounce it.

'All done?' asks a pretty face from the open door. Her eyes are wide and blue, and her hair long and blonde—essential accoutrements for all receptionists. 'They're ready for you now.'

'Yes, all done, and now I'm *ter'war*-fied,' I say, fishing. She gives me a blank look. I try again with even more emphasis on how the French might pronounce the word: still nothing.

She sweeps the test sheets from the desk, spins on particularly spectacular ankles and swishes her palomino mane out through the doorway. I skip along behind and try to keep up.

There are six of them. Three each side of an oblong conference table. All but one must have left high school early to come and interview me. The other is a handsome woman in her mid-thirties. She looks elegant in a tasteful outfit. Her warm smile gives me hope that she is a possible ally. A young man with a neatly trimmed, darkly confident beard scans the test sheets. Without looking up he points to an empty chair at the end of the table. I sit.

'You were close,' he says, showing bright white teeth through dark wiry hair. "There is no English equivalent to the French word 'ter'war.' It means many things: area, soil, region, and flavours in wine imparted by nature etc., so *terra firma* is a pretty good guess.'

Pretty good guess—cheeky bugger!

His eyes droop sadly. 'But it is a Cabernet Sauvignon, not Shiraz,' he lingers long on the 'z'.

The panel is efficient. Each has a role. One makes introductions then another asks questions about my background and foreground. We discuss the current state of the wine industry: the effects of the drought, the glut of grapes, and pesky imports. I hold my own thanks to some expert advice from a brother-in-law who is a wine marketing consultant.

'Your interview piece is very interesting.' The condescending tones are coming from a very erect young girl to my right. 'But why did you write it in *that* way?'

I study her upturned nose, 'In ... *what* way?'

'That ... question and answer interview style ... it just simply won't do for our magazine.'

Oh really?

I explain I am a stranger to Norm Walker. He expected questions he could give specific answers to—probably to make sure *I* got it right. 'And as for that style,' I add, 'the format is from a fairly well-known magazine called *Vogue*.'

Their eyes glow ghostly phosphorescence and dart around the table to connect and confirm between them, without words, that this old fart has stepped out of line.

Children of the corn

They scribble furiously on their notepads.

Whoops

The handsome older woman neither darts nor scribbles. The erect young girl promises to send me a copy of the next issue of the magazine and I know the interview is over. I will not be wine cadet of the year.

∞

'I couldn't tell the Cabernet from the Shir-a … or the terr-a, from the ter'wa.'

We are leaning on his wheelie bin contemplating the profusion of leaves raked into neat piles around his feet. It is a blustery day and the leaves refuse to behave.

'They were kids, Norm. They looked twelve but were probably in their twenties with kids of their own.'

'What are you going to do now?'

'I haven't a clue,' I said.

18

The presence of the past

He is a tall man with that full head of thick, white hair and the stature of the athlete he once was. The presence of the past still sits with him. On the night of his 80th birthday he leaves the house where he was born to cross the street to where he now lives. Unsteadily, he mounts the kerb and enters the dimly lit carport. In that moment two shadows merge. The man he used to be appears out of the darkness and suffuses the form of the man he is now. Strong, cheerful and cocky, the young Norm smiles as he takes the old Norm home.

I watch until he is safely inside.

It was a night filled with stories. His stories and mine, in the house his father built. I showed him singed floorboards in one of the front rooms and he related his earliest memory.

He was five or six years old, walking up Penfold Road from the tram stop, holding his mother's hand, when a young girl came running down the hill towards them. The house was on fire. He looked up the hill to see his dad and some men from the winery fighting the blaze. And although he was afraid for his dad, he secretly hoped his Meccano set[15] was safe.

The clothes iron had been left on and it had burnt through the table, igniting the timber floor, and then the house. Norm's mum reasoned that his dad had accidentally switched the iron on when he came home for lunch. But Norm always believed his father went along with that story just to keep the peace. I ask if the young girl was his older sister Joyce. But he isn't sure.

He talks about 1951 when the vines in the Grange vineyard were to be replaced. Peas were planted in the interim to prepare the soil and infuse it with nitrogen. The peas attracted many birds that he took pot shots at with a shotgun from his office window. And, with a voice filled with regret, he tells me a story of ring-necked parrots. They never left one of their own in trouble: never left one behind. If you shot one you shot them all.

Stories and moods ebb and flow and blend as I relate my own stories and regrets about shooting wildlife in my teenage years.

We have become close since the interview some months ago. He invites me to the gatherings in the den to play snooker and meet his friends. I can't always go but he asks just the same. I soon learn that the rumble of thunder I hear across Ormond Avenue on Thursday nights is the collective hammering of pool cues on a wooden floor—in praise of exceptionally skilful shots or equally exceptional shots that are just pure arse. The tribal chants and hammering and howls in a war-dance of older men celebrating life: letting the world know they are still around.

Cakes have been baked and books exchanged. I have met Norm Walker's family and he has met mine. On the night of his eightieth birthday, we talked about the past and the present and about what you lose as you grow older.

Norm Walker is a man who clings to the past to compensate for the things that are changing around him, things that disappear with age: old friends, the ability to play golf or tennis and the status of the renowned athlete he enjoyed as a younger man. But he keeps the links connected. He works hard to maintain friendships and bonds forged over many years. He is the host, the master of ceremonies. He has lived in Magill all his life and he keeps a lifetime of stories alive. His stories tessellate his life and give him symmetry.

His is a life-path worth sharing.

So, on the night of his 80th birthday, I tell Norm Walker I want to write a book set in present-day Magill, and I would like him to be the central character. He is surprised and eager to begin. We both agree that our quest should start the very next day.

19

Driving Miss Daisy

'I'll drive,' he said, 'so I can stop whenever I want.'

He sounds nervous as he backs the car out. We leave Ormond Avenue and turn into Penfold Road.

'I just want to get a feel for the place, Norm.'

He pulls himself forward in the seat using the steering wheel for leverage, and waggles his head in the general direction of Penfold's winery as we enter The Parade roundabout.

'Hang on! ... Wait! ... Woo oh! ... Look out!' I squeal. Norm takes the roundabout too fast while looking everywhere but at the road. We bump then mount the concrete kerb, bounce across the roundabout and drop onto the road on the far side. I flail about in my seat, all arms and legs, garrotted by the seat belt. Norm ignores my girlie screams and continues his monologue without missing a beat.

'This is what they now call Penfolds Magill Estate,' he says, 'but it was the original Grange vineyard.'

He drives onto the estate.

Grange Hermitage became so popular that the single-source vineyard couldn't cope with demand. Max named the wine Grange Hermitage after a region in France. The grape variety is Shiraz or Syrah as it is known in France (Norm was saying Syrah when I thought he was saying Shirá.) The name Hermitage identified the single-source vineyard in Magill and added a little prestige. But when the edict came down that the French regions could no longer be used to name wines produced outside of the areas, Grange Hermitage became Grange and Champagne became sparkling wine.

'It's still great wine, but Hermitage was the original,' says Norm.

The car is moving much slower now and Norm points to the old Penfold homestead. His voice sounds far away. We have left the constant drone of traffic behind and we are now in another place. It could easily be a vineyard in Europe. The homestead is a gift, a glimpse of living history, uniquely Australian.

Norm is having a conversation with himself.

'Doctor Rawson Penfold ... have I got that wrong? Rawson Penfold? I could be wrong. 'Rawson ... Rawson, I think it was Rawson.'

It has to be a challenge for him. So many years have passed and so many changes have taken place; he may not have talked about any of this for a long time.

'This is the Grange Cottage,' he continues. 'I thought we could look through it with a friend who works here, Johnny Bird, if he's available. I'll have to make an appointment for that though,' he adds quickly.

He drives the car up to a cluster of older buildings and then turns back in the direction we came.

'Those buildings are original,' he says.

'What ... built by Rawson Penfold?' I ask.

'Eh?'

Louder this time: 'Would they have been built by Dr Penfold?'

'*1844 to Evermore*,'[16] he laughs. 'Who was around in 1844? I don't know who built them ... I can't tell you that.'

Jesus. No more stupid questions then.

The vista opens before us as we drive back to the entrance. I try to imagine a time when the vines provided a platform of glorious views all the way to the sea, many kilometres in the distance. The elevation is perfect. The land cascades to the horizon with barely a bump on the way.

It seems the more Norm talks the more he remembers. I can tell he surprises himself with some of his recollections. He becomes a host to the past as he invites it to join us in the present.

A cyclist is crossing the opening to Penfold Road. He is middle-aged, overweight and his body is encased in Lycra. We watch his progress. Bulging, basketball sized buttocks threaten to break free from the confines of the sausage-tight Lycra skin. The indicator light on the dashboard clicks a rhythm to his swaying backside. He makes his way slowly across the windscreen, red-faced and sweaty, as we sit in restrained silence.

Opposite stands a stately looking home the Penfold family once owned. Norm remembers that the garage at the back held five or six cars which included a Maserati and a car he thought may have been called a Hispano.

We accelerate uphill on Penfold Road heading south. Norm is getting into his stride. His head swivels as if on a stick as he looks in all directions.

He is like a passenger on a tour bus: pointing while talking, rotating in his seat, pushing visual memory to the limit, and arguing with himself as the changes in the landscape play havoc with his script of memories. What he fails to realise is—*he's driving.*

'There was a big hedge all along there and Stonyfell vines were on this side of the road, and Penfold vines were along the other side over there,' he turns and points at both sides, 'all the way down to Kensington Road.'

We circumnavigate cars parked by the side of the road and careen along our merry way. Up ahead, another roundabout looms.

Should I say something? He'll see it, won't he?

The car glides into the roundabout in silence and exits gracefully on the other side. I pull my fingertips from the indentations in the dashboard, and, feeling a little embarrassed, ask, 'What was along this bit here then?' Norm clears his throat and describes an olive tree plantation and wild olive trees that were abundant in the area. And then he shows me the spot where James Crompton's olive oil factory had been.

As a boy Norm picked wild olives during the holidays and the Cromptons paid him one pound[17] a bag. He was amazed that a bag of wild olives could be worth so much money.

We make our way to the Stonyfell winery built on the hillside above Stonyfell Road. Norm explains how some older wineries were purposely built on hillsides for gravity flow to run the juices downhill.

My mind's eye pictures a hillside stained by thick purple juice gushing from beneath the vines above a Willy Wonka Winery. His description was more feasible: from the crusher to the fermentation tanks and, once fermented, downhill again to the next stage in the process.

'They didn't have many pumps back then,' he adds.

Gandy's Gully is wild scrub, rock formations and olive trees and a favourite adventure playground for Norm the schoolboy. He points to a spot and recounts the story of the underground tank that had frogs at the bottom. There was always a large bull in the paddock but Norm and his friends had to have those frogs. He could still see the bull clearly. It would glare at them as they waved their arms, made faces and jeered from behind the protection of the fence. Eventually, the bull got bored and moved away. The boys then took the risk, in a nervous rush across the paddock and down a ladder to the bottom of the tank.

'Getting out was the hard part,' says Norm.

Frogs covered in slime and wet with black mud wriggled and croaked inside the boys' shirts and trouser pockets as they peeked above the rim of the tank. If the bull was close it had the upper hand in a game each side had played many times. The bull looked at their anxious faces as it snorted and stomped an impressive and terrifying reply to their earlier antics. After showing them who was boss, the bull became bored once more and shuffled off.

'The second that bull moved,' said Norm, 'we were up the ladder and running like buggery.'

Our jaunt takes us into Grevillea Crescent where a golf course once existed. Grevillea Crescent is a place of beauty: of splendid homes and a nature reserve called Heatherbank that was once part of the Grey Box forest that covered the Adelaide Plains. Spider orchids and other wildflowers grew on the forest floor for thousands of years, and they survive today because of the gentle care of Dr Moxon Simpson and his wife Elizabeth. We stop to look. I wind down the window, inhale the sweet tang of wildflowers and listen closely for an ancient echo of forest sounds. The air is whisper-quiet and so are we. Norm looks up the street.

'The first tee was over there,' he points out; 'this was all golf links, it was boggy and marshy then and you could have bought the lot for a song—if you could sing.'

A house had been built too close to the fairway on the ladies' course. So the fairway was altered to accommodate the incursion, and the ladies played around the house, as some ladies do.

I was away with the spider orchids: lost in the Grey Box forest.

On leaving Grevillea Crescent we traverse the main road once again. A turbo-charged something or other impatiently spits and hisses its way past with an aggressive burst of speed. The young man driving gives us a filthy look for having the audacity to slow his progress to nowhere. The traffic banks-up suddenly and 'turbo Timmy' has to brake hard to stop in time. Norm smiles and continues. He speaks of thick blankets of vines that once covered the area. The endless rows were a sight he took for granted, but now misses.

We turn off Kensington Road into the wide, gumtree-lined Edgcumbe Terrace. This was once a narrow dirt track between the vines, a favourite spot for shooting hares and foxes. Now Edgcumbe Terrace resembles many other streets in the neighbourhood, long and wide with large, plush-looking homes nestled either side of a black strap of bitumen. In Norm's time that space between the vines was also a notorious parking spot for what he politely calls 'illicit affairs.'

In the dark of night, when the spotlights swept the vines, shadowy silhouettes could be seen behind the fogged glass of cars parked at prudent intervals along the track. When the shotguns barked and boomed and the hares and foxes dashed and darted erratically in and out of the vines, other hares and foxes dashed and darted erratically in and out of the dark depths of back seats. Heads froze in steamy windows. Then in a flurry of bare flesh, panic stricken faces and clutched clothing, engines roared as cars vanished into the night.

Norm laughs triumphantly.

I see the beams of light criss-crossing in the dust and raking the dark sky as the cars snake away, fishtailing along the narrow track.

Many of the streets are named after varieties of wine: Grange and Dalwood, Muscat and Shiraz. Street after street it becomes difficult to imagine the landscape without houses. We are locked in suburbia looking for a way out. Houses are the new landscape and always will be. Then suddenly we are back where we began. Norm nods wistfully at the majestic stone building on the corner of The Parade and Penfold Road. 'That's where I spent my days,' he says. We enter the round-about once more, this time with grace. He drives slowly past the building. It is a time-honoured landmark, fronted by spectacular pines, immense columns of foliage that mushroom into the sky.

We soar upwards above the vines, up onto the tiers on Coach Road. Norm's large, early-model Holden sedan has a floating motion that intensifies the euphoria I begin to feel.

You're the best driver in the world, Norm.

What I see is stunning. The deep incision of Gandy's Gully now lies far below. The rounded curves of the hillsides take on human shapes as each folds and envelopes in and out of the other, moulding gullies that ripple across the breadth of the ranges. My peripheral vision is all-encompassing—180 degrees without turning my head is not impossible up here. And the sky is a dome of deep blue. Maybe this is why we seek out high places: to lift our eyes from the streets, to seek perspective on everyday life.

We are very high up in a narrow street. Norm squeezes the car to my side of the road to allow a large truck to thump past from the opposite direction.

'We used to sledge down these hills on barrel staves,' he grins.

From the passenger's seat the world disappears over the very lip of the road. I look down. Below me a swimming pool, pristine and inviting, sits on a precipice: beyond it, nothing.

An image of Norm Walker, downhill racer, on a sledge made from the staves of wine barrels, laughing maniacally as he tears down a snowless slope, flashes into my mind. My fingertips seek the indents on the dashboard once more and I look at him. His eyes urge me to feel the thrill.

He's having a bit of fun with me.

'Look how steep it is,' he goads.

Okay ... okay ... I'm ... looking ... I'm looking.

'We had absolutely no control. We just went like hell and hoped for the best.'

Curve by curve we make our way back down, and the views are breathtaking. I live five minutes away but had never seen any of this.

I wonder when Norm was last up here. These hills gather around him like a comfortable old blanket. He knows every dip and twist in the winding road, and at each bend another story unfolds.

We sweep a long curve at the mouth of a gully where an entrepreneur and novice farmer, Bertram Cox, once attempted to build a dam. Bertram was the willing type, willing to try anything. But beneath the smattering of topsoil in the gully lay bedrock. The water seeped through and Bertram's dam never held a drop.

'*Farming is fun,*' said Norm. 'You can read all about Bertram Cox in a book called, *Farming is Fun.*'

Another curve brings us to a signboard that reads:

> Stone Mine Reserve: unstable mines and quarries in this reserve; do not enter any mines. The paths are Class 3 walking trails. Natural hazards, steep slopes, unstable surfaces, minor water crossings, and snakes in warm weather.

So if you slip on the unstable surfaces you will plummet down the steep slopes, breaking many bones on the way, and end up face down in water next to a minor crossing where you will probably drown. If not, then a warm snake will put you out of your misery.

In Norm Walker's time this gully existed for the imaginations of young boys looking for adventures that would test their mettle.

'When you read that sign it's a wonder we didn't kill ourselves'.

They played in the devil's cauldron and didn't know it. The danger never occurred to them. Danger was the allure of perilous play. They spent Saturdays on the slopes with their sledges and a box of nails for repairs.

The downhill sledge juggernaut began above a steep gradient that pitched and dipped to one side. It was chosen as the route most likely to negotiate a way through the dense olive groves on the lower slopes. The sledge had no steering mechanism. Your fate was left to judgement, luck and French oak. If your judgement was good you went between the trees, and if you were lucky the staves held together. If neither of these things happened then you bailed out early and took a tumble, sliding on your backside through the stubble down the stone covered escarpment while your sledge hit an olive tree.

His voice conveyed the stories, but he was somewhere else, outside himself, feeling the memory. Maybe that's what memories are. An aura of feeling that surrounds you that draws you out from time to time while your being continues in automation.

'No helmets, pads, brakes or wheels — I'd call that an extreme sport, Norm.'

'Nah ... it was just bloody good fun.'

We meander through the streets on the hillsides and consider the large homes on spacious allotments that replaced the vines that replaced the stringy bark forests: lavish mansions where the hard rubbish on the footpath in front of your house is also a measure of your wealth.

'Those lamps look pretty good,' says Norm. 'Why don't you grab them and give them to your wife for Mother's Day.'

I laugh, but he stops the car so I put the lamps in the boot. A few weeks later they become part of my own hard rubbish collection. They did add a brief period of prestige to the neighbourhood's estimation of my wealth.

We pass the Penfold chimney on the way back down: an obelisk in the hillside. I look at the homestead amongst the vines where wispy traces of Christopher and Mary Penfold still linger. We pass the old stone winery where Norm 'spent his days' and sail around our mulberry bush of a roundabout and down Penfold Road.

'Méthode champenoise.' Two words break the silence. Norm pronounces the words, 'met-tod sham-pen-whaz.'

My head wobbles in his direction. 'Whaaat ...' I drag the word out of me. Going up the downs and round the rounds has reduced me to jelly. He repeats himself, only this time he curls his lips around the beautiful French words, savouring each, rolling and smacking them off his tongue with as much relish as he can muster—'méth...ode champ...en...oise.'

'French vignerons taught my father how to make champagne by the traditional method; *méthode champenoise* they call it. They called it champagne, so we called it champagne. Now it's sparkling wine.'

'How does it go again, Norm … met…tod shimp…pan…zeze?' I was keen to get it right. It would be the third deposit in my wine-words-to-use-at-parties dictionary, after meniscus and before terroir.

He leans forward to the rear view mirror pursing and jutting his lips. I do the same. And together we purse and jut in the mirror rolling the words around our mouths, tasting the sounds until I get it right: méthode champenoise. We sit back in our seats, satisfied. *I hope no-one was watching that little French lesson.*

Our tour continues, as peppertrees on Penfold Road become markers for Norm to measure the past magnitude and scope of the vineyards. He recalls a Muscat vineyard opposite his father's house. The sweet, dark purple fruit that hung in the leafy green was irresistible to small children passing by. Norm remembers his own children, at a very young age, bringing home a bucket full of Shiraz grapes from the Grange vineyard so he could show them how to make wine.

I try to imagine the sinuous flow of vines sweeping downhill to the village. What did they look like when they weren't lush and green? Leafless, gnarled and twisted stumps in rows like grotesque muscular scarecrows, or ranks of dead soldiers entangled in wire on a battlefield.

The row of pepper trees begins to peter out. Their hanging dreadlocks swish over the verge as we stop by the kerb. Behind the trees a sign on a fence reads, 'Home Park Lodge'. Norm leans to my side of the car and points. 'There used to be a little winery in there.'

20

Time in the sun

The ingredients in the cake called Magill are a resonant blend of characters and their moments of time in the sun. The mix is complex and can sometimes be at variance with the recipe, as baking a cake can be. But with care the cake rises and reveals its splendour.

Magill today is redolent with what has gone before.

In 1866 E. W. Wright planted vines, built a wine cellar and residence and called his property Home Park. Joseph Crompton owned the property twice, once in 1874 and again in 1883.[18] Mrs Crompton planted the first pepper trees in South Australia with seeds she brought from Spain. The trees still flourish today.

As the story goes, land available to ordinary citizens was mostly crown land on perpetual lease. As no contract is legal unless there is an exchange of value, contracts were written up as one peppercorn per annum: an Alice in Wonderland quirk of British eccentricity.

Peppercorn trees are not native to South Australia. They are native to the Andes in South America. So the imaginative Mrs Crompton made sure there were ample peppercorns available to those in need of rental accommodation. How long does a pepper tree live? The nearest guess is 400 years. But whatever the age, Mrs Crompton's time in the sun will live with the trees.

Fast-forward to 1969.

John Dillon was a self-confessed stickybeak. He was also a heavy smoker. The last cigarette he ever smoked was a costly one. He lit one up as he ambled along Romalo Avenue on a sun-filled May morning in 1969. With not a penny in his pocket and with no intentions of spending what he did not have, he made his way to Penfold Road. Equal measures of fate, curiosity and a whim were luring him that morning to a moment of time in the sun.

As a surveyor, the division and subdivision of land fascinated John. It was a passion. History was precisely measured and meticulously recorded in survey maps and plans. The early surveyors used nib, ink and blotter to scratch and divide the land in lines across a page, each depiction a story of life in a space upon the surface. Sections and allotments were numbered and compartmentalised in inches and degrees. Signatures and initials, docket numbers and dates recorded the dealings and doings of the inhabitants of Magill. Lots were bought then sold, then bought back again. The maps and plans were a traceable, linear testimony to the life and times of the landowners.

John checked his watch; he was early. There was still plenty of time to have a good look at the place before the auction got underway. With the manner and poise of a real buyer, he smiled and nodded a brisk good morning to the agent at the gate, who quickly handed him a leaflet. A little make-believe never hurt anybody. According to the information, 31 Penfold Road was the original Home Park residence. A gracious home, comprising eight spacious rooms, set on one acre of land. The prestigious property had a 138-foot frontage to Penfold Road and 148 feet to Pepper Street at the rear, with a total depth of 306 feet front to back. John ran an experienced eye corner to corner and front to back before accepting the figures. Then he mingled with the crowd inside the grand home.

In the back yard he stepped down into a layer of time—down into the other Magill, into 6,000 square feet of the past. Yellow lights shimmered and dotted the dusky glow-worm atmosphere of the immense cellar. Dust-covered bottles, never to be cleaned, sat silent in stone and brick and timber. He could find room to keep some favourites down here. Maybe Maxi Schubert would provide a Grange or two as a wager on their next round of golf.

John was lost in his daydream when a voice on the stairs beckoned all buyers. He began to wonder what it would be like to own this slice of the past.

The bidding was slow, then fast. The group consisted mostly of men, so innate competitiveness and a glorious wine cellar obliterated all common sense. As the bids passed the high twenties John felt a shiver of excitement. He was enjoying himself: time for a smoke. With a well-practised pitch he confidently flicked a cigarette up into his mouth. The auctioneer pointed the gavel at him and said, 'Thank you sir, $31,000.'

John left. He tiptoed through the crowd and snuck out through the gate beneath the pepper trees. Their spindly green fingers tugged at his hair and his arms in an effort to stop him. He crossed Penfold Road, with the auctioneer at his heels. John strode out swiftly in long determined strides up Romalo Ave towards the safety of home. But he could not dodge destiny. He cursed the dreaded weed, bloody cigarettes. John stopped and turned to face his fate, expecting a horde of bidders to be gathered in the middle of the road preparing to bid for his blood. What would the neighbours think?

But the auctioneer was alone.

The happy cigarette flick had taken the bidding to $31,000. The previous bid had been a 'dummy' one, made on behalf of the seller of the property. A risky practice used to keep the bidders' bidding. It had not worked. The owners were now more than eager to accept the $31,000 that John did not have, but they would be kind enough to allow him time to find it. The property was 31 Penfold Road. The price was $31,000. The deposit was $3,100 and his present address was 31 Romalo Ave. He was trapped by numerology.

John made a pledge to give up smoking. His last cigarette turned out to be the most expensive but the best he ever smoked.

The machinations of money gathering are an art form, a talent John Dillon discovered through determination and some good luck. The circumstances of his life changed on the flick of a cigarette and provided an opportunity he would not let slip away. Within a few months he moved his family into Home Park, his slice of the past, his slice of the cake of history.

And as the mélange of our cake mix is kneaded, more names surface ... then blend ... surface ... then blend: Jean-Francois Galaup La Perouse; Léon Edmond Mazure, and Hurtle Frank Walker.

21

Jarrah

Remember that what you are told is really threefold: shaped by the teller, reshaped by the listener, concealed from both by the dead man of the tale.[19]

'Are you sure that's him, Norm?'
'That's the one he always said was him.'

'The one in the middle at the back looks like Nick. Maybe *that's* him.'

'No ... no ... he's in front of the bloke who has his arms folded, on the right.'

'How do you get a nickname like Jarrah from Hurtle Frank Walker?'

'I have no idea,' says Norm.

The 'Boys in the Vines' photograph is one of those rare images that is so real it makes you believe the past did exist. It allows imagination to cross the threshold between the present and the past. The photographer has interrupted a working day to capture the scene. But it is taken when the wagon is full. And the looks on the faces of the pickers give the impression their break is being encroached upon: one smile only, from a bearded man in the background. You can almost hear the clanking of the metal buckets and the screeching of the handles being lowered as the boys, uncomfortably, ready themselves for the shot. The drooping moustache and drooping features of the man with the basket on his head indicate the basket is heavy with grapes, forcing his neck into his torso as the *damn photographer fiddles for far too long with the bloody camera*. A few of the boys are pudgy well-fed. One of the older boys standing at the back looks Italian, and coupled with the hat he's wears could pass for Chico Marx.[20] The boy beside him exudes defiance and impatience, with his hands on his hips.

Of the ten boys in the vines only four survive World War One.[21] The boy standing on the right at the end of the front row survived. The boy's name is Hurtle Frank Walker but his mates called him Jarrah. I search the face of 12-year-old Jarrah, looking for the essence of the boy who became Hurtle Walker the man. He seems shy, a little self-conscious, as though he would give anything to be doing something other than having his picture taken.

Jarrah is the name of the dark-red wood of a large Western Australian tree that attracts many adjectives: hardy, robust, strong, resilient and long-lasting.

The word jarrah is entrenched in the Australian psyche. It evokes a sense of 'Australianness' and unique Australian characteristics: enduring, faithful, loyal and true. Could they be the traits someone saw in Hurtle Walker, the boy, traits in a nickname that would forge his character for life?

Life is made of minute details such as these.

The boy nicknamed Jarrah lived in a different time. He lived in a time of serious and pragmatic people who were only a generation removed from the first settlers in Magill. The faces of the pickers in the photograph don't exactly reflect the romantic notions or the revered ethos we place on wine in modern times. Singing to the vines would not have been a priority during a tough eleven-hour day in 1902. But the boys preferred the hard labour to going to school. Jarrah was a dab hand at grape picking from the age of ten. And with a shortage of manpower in Magill at the time, boy power was in great demand. The boys negotiated exemptions from school and wages were settled at seven shillings and sixpence per week.

After a value-for-labour analysis, using calculations from sophisticated software and allowing for the current deficit and Goods and Services Tax, ten-year-old boys in the 21st century could conclude that seven shillings and sixpence for an eleven-hour day, five days a week, was slave labour. And they would consider the equivalent in wages today not worth getting off the couch for, or interrupting an all-action video game on a wide-screen TV.

That is not to say fun did not exist in a boy's life in Jarrah's time.

Jarrah's playground was unique. He could get lost in adventures along the tracks in the hills not far from his front door. He could climb

the trees that were part of the ancient, giant gum tree forest by Third
Creek. Or he could explore the crumbling huts and shanties along its
banks, built to shelter early settlers like his grandparents. He could
search for the sites and re-live the stories of the strange rituals
performed by natives around blazing camp fires near his house. And if
none of that took his fancy, there was always the flagpole in the
schoolyard on Pepper Street, a short walk from Ellis Street, the street
where he was born.

The school flagpole was a long, coarse, stringy bark sapling. But the
climb was worth it. From the top he had spectacular views over the
land. Uninterrupted lines of sight to the sea where the silhouettes of
ships anchored at Largs Bay shimmered in the distant blue. Or he
could look across the teeming, orderly rows of grapevines that
swarmed over the land and into the folds of the hillsides. This was his
place, his home. Hurtle 'Jarrah' Walker lived and worked in Magill all
his life. He moved only once: a kilometre away from where he was
born.

He was the only boy in school who could climb to the top of that
flagpole. Whenever the hoisting apparatus failed, as it often did, he
was official flag monitor on days of special significance. On Thursday
the 26th of April 1900,[22] troopers from the South Australian contin-
gent of the Australian Imperial Regiment paraded past the school at
midday. They were on their way to meet the Governor at his summer
residence in Marble Hill before embarking on a campaign to the Boer
War in South Africa. It was a challenging day for a flag monitor, who
had not only been sent up the flagpole to attach and unfurl the flag,
but also given strict instructions to bring down the decorative item
that had mysteriously appeared at the top of the pole … on that day of
significance.

Imagine the scene …

Hurtle could hear the commotion before he got to Pepper Street. As he turned the corner he saw a small crowd gathered around the flagpole in front of the schoolhouse. Mrs Service, from Howitt's Bakehouse, was standing next to the headmaster, Mr Rowley. She was clutching her pulpy stomach in a futile attempt to stop it from jiggling; her face glowed red in the early morning sun as she laughed uncontrollably. Mr Rowley, however, was not laughing.

Hurtle squinted up at the flagpole. The morning sun had just peeked over the hilltops and was shining like a beacon. He cupped his hands around his eyes and could now see what all the fuss was about. A gleaming white porcelain chamber pot, adorned with posies of tiny bluebells, was perched on top of the flagpole. Hurtle looked at the crowd. Knowing grins told him they were eager to see what would happen next—perhaps a little corporal punishment? He looked at the headmaster's scowl.

'My office Walker ... now,' Mr Rowley hissed.

A parade was a rare treat for children living an almost rural existence in the Magill of 1900, especially for young boys, whose imaginations would sail over the oceans to ride at full charge with the troopers in battle across the wide savannahs of the Transvaal.

Standing in front of the old schoolhouse, it is not difficult to imagine the scene. At midday the shrill wail of the whistle at Penfold's and the muted clanging of the school bell dismisses the children for lunch and heralds the coming of the troops. Minus the all-pervading traffic noise of the 21st century, sound carried far and wide across silent landscapes: over the vines, into the streets and down Magill Road to greet the troopers. Shopkeepers and locals line the roadway. Men wave their hats and caps and women wave lace handkerchiefs. Children dart in and out of line to look down the dusty track, desperate to be the

first to spot them. Bartenders and ostlers and regulars from the
World's End Inn crowd the inn's rickety balcony above the street. An
early keg or hogshead tapped for the occasion could easily see the
revellers ride the old balcony to the ground with glee.

I can hear the troopers coming ...

*The lead horseman looks magnificent. He holds a long lance with a small
triangular flag at the top. The base of the lance is cupped in a leather pouch
on the saddle just below his knee. The breeze ruffles the striking feather
fastened to the upturned side of his hat. He is broad-shouldered and handsome, his skin the colour of copper. Traces of a faint moustache are visible
and the ladies in the crowd smile and wave excitedly to get his attention.*

*Despite a light coating of dust, the leather belt across his body glints in the
bright sunlight. The looped curves of a sword handle are visible at his side.
The decorative burnished silver stock jangles in its metal scabbard.*

*Trooper and horse are moulded as one. The horse snorts and paws at tiny
dust swirls on the road then prances and dances sideways. He is a big animal,
around 16 or 17 hands, and solid. The legs are thick and strong, not spindly
like the thoroughbred. His chestnut-coloured flanks glisten with sweat as he
struts by. The rest of the troopers follow behind. They all look alike, young
and strong and proud. The crowd cheers. Hurtle can barely breathe.*

It must have set Jarrah's imagination on fire: war horses, rugged
and ready for battle, where survival would depend on the strength of
both horse and rider.

Horses were highly valued in those times. Knowing how to ride
and handle horses was second nature to boys born in nineteenth-
century Magill. Horses were a necessity, but could be just as exciting as

a BMX, skateboard or a quad bike is to boys today. Regular deliveries of meat, groceries and postal items were made on horseback to outlying properties. The excitement came when gates were closed. Over the top the boys would fly, sometimes losing their cargo in the dirt. If the delivery was meat it got a quick rinsing in Third Creek before being handed over to the customer with a smile. Percy Sutton, the village butcher, could not understand why some customers complained that his chops, while tender and delicious, were sometimes a little gritty.

Horses figure large in the later life of Hurtle Walker: in his bravery in war and in the life of his daughter Joyce, who had a great love of horses.

The parade passes by. I gaze uphill as the ghostly regiment fades away. I can see the local gardeners scooping up the horse dung like gold from the streets, before it too disappears.

My imagination returns to the schoolyard ...
Mr Howitt from Howitt's Bakehouse next door is already in the yard surrounded by a pack of excited young faces. He is holding a large sugar bag above their heads. They know what is in the bag. On days of special celebration he fills the bag with all the sticky sweet delicacies that Mrs Service can bake. The children jostle for position. It's a bun scramble; and it's not for the faint-hearted.
Mr Howitt dips frantically and the frenzy increases:

> *Fresh rolls and finger buns and jam curls on cakes,*
> *Cream buns and cupcakes and mince pies fresh-baked*
> *With cream on their faces and jam in their hair*
> *They scramble for the buns in the dust without a care (Neill 2010).*

As he slowly pulls the last, stickiest jam bun from the bag, the chaos subsides and turns to silent anticipation. Mr Howitt lifts the bun with dramatic effect high above his head. The children wait. He leans back and cocks his arm ready to throw. The children squeal, and then fall about laughing as the last bun disappears into Mr Howitt's mouth. The scramble is over.

When Hurtle Walker left primary school at 14, he had completed seven years of schooling and like most boys of that era, 14 was the transition age of 'boys to men,' an age to find steady work to help support the family during the hard years of the early twentieth century.

The foundations of Hurtle Walker's family were laid in Devonshire, England.

George Walker and Maria 'Mary' Coulson married around 1848, migrated to Australia and built a hut on the banks of Third Creek at Woodforde, near Magill. George and Mary had 10 children: Tom, Mary Elizabeth, George, Minute, John, Lois, Alfred, Annie, Ellen and Emma. Alfred died at six years-of-age and Emma at ten months. Their remaining children lived fulfilling lives. The matriarch of the family, Maria 'Mary' Walker, lived until 27 March 1896, and the patriarch, George Walker, died on 27 February 1901, when Hurtle Walker was ten.

George and Mary's son, John Walker, married New Zealand-born Henrietta Ward on 20 September 1882, at the Baptist church in Norton Summit near Magill. Henrietta gave birth to 11 children: Horace John, Mabel Rose, Edith Gertrude, Edith Gertrude,[23] Arthur John, Hurtle Frank, Norman George, Doris Evelyn, Edgar Ward, Leonard Ward and Percy Walker. Of their 11 children only five survived: Mabel Rose, Arthur John, Hurtle Frank, Norman George and Leonard Ward Walker.[24]

It was a time of high infant mortality, on a scale incomprehensible to the modern world. How did parents cope? How did siblings cope? How did it affect Hurtle Walker? His brother Percy was the last to be born and then lost, at ten days old in 1897. Hurtle was seven when Percy died, a schoolboy in his second year of school.

I could not find the graves: all the little children; all the lonely bones.

So by the age of 14 Jarrah's work ethic was well-honed in the vineyards. He knew much about hard work, life and death as did many youths back then. These were the formative years, the years his character would be established as he left Jarrah the boy behind, to face life as Hurtle Walker the man.

22

The vivacious little Gaul

'... In the cellar we sampled the sparkling cup, sparkling burgundy and claret, and ate Monsieur's excellently pickled olives, and felt peacefully inclined to the world...' [25]

Five years before Hurtle Walker (left) was born, French vigneron Léon Edmond Mazure (right) made Magill his home.

Ernest Wittington was not only a meticulous wine reporter for the *Adelaide Observer* newspaper; he was also a writer with a creative imagination and a fine turn of phrase to his prose. He greatly admired and was enamoured of Léon Edmond Mazure's personality and his inventive and tactile talents. Wittington hailed him the 'vivacious little Gaul' in tribute to his winemaking skills, tenacity, and probably the French spirit he epitomised that connected the cradle of European winemaking to Magill.

Léon Edmond Mazure was an artisan who dedicated his life to the perfection of grand wines. His many notable triumphs include St Henri claret and the first Australian style Sparkling Burgundy. French ships would wait patiently at anchor in Port Adelaide for deliveries of Mazure's St Henri Claret. The news that it was a 'good drop' travelled far. The ten-hour journey from Magill to the port by bullock wagon only improved the taste. St Henri is still in that exceptional class of red wines produced by Penfolds Wines today. Who was the first vigneron to make Sparkling Burgundy? That dispute still keeps South Australian and Victorian intercolonial rivalry very much alive. There are reams written on the Sparkling Burgundy dispute between the two states. What is important is that Léon Mazure got it right. He created an Australian Burgundy that was 'big and gutsy' from Shiraz grapes that came from A. P. Birks in Clare, north of Adelaide. Grapes that made wine that was so 'big' that sometimes it had to be broken down first.[26] Another of Léon Mazure's notable triumphs was one that would determine the life-path of a 14-year-old boy named Hurtle Walker.

Léon was manager of the Auldana winery in Magill when Hurtle first picked grapes in the vineyards. Mazure was impressed by Hurtle. He recognised the traits that earned Walker the nickname Jarrah and offered him a full-time job. Hurtle's day began at seven am. He bought two packets of cigarettes and the morning paper for his new boss and delivered them to the Mazure family home. He fed the chickens and escorted Mazure's youngest son, Emil, safely to Mary and Janey Mercer's private school, Hillsee, a mile from the Mazure home.

The rest of his day was spent working at the wine cellars at anything that was going until it was time to pick up Emil. After seeing Emil safely home, Hurtle fed the fowls their second meal of the day and returned to the cellars to work until 6:00 pm, often by candlelight. His salary was now a hefty nine shillings per week.

The Mazures were by then established residents of Magill. They were also French. Interacting with the Mazure family would influence Hurtle Walker and open his mind to other worlds and other possibilities. He saw much of Mazure's family life, especially at breakfast, as they readied themselves for the day ahead. What did they eat for breakfast? It may have been croissants, delicate pastries, crepes and strong coffee, much as we imagine all French breakfasts to be. A Magill boy's cultural delicacy was a hot yeast bun with a gooey, melted, chocolate frog in the centre. In early Magill, French delicacies would not have been readily available from the local bakery. Léon Mazure's wife, Henrietta, may have baked traditional French fare that filled the house with exotic aromas. Either way, Hurtle would absorb another culture: the food, the accents and the French language, spoken in the home to maintain their mother tongue and connections to homeland.

Perhaps the first morning went something like this ...

Hurtle arrives just as the family are sitting down to breakfast. The breakfast aromas in the Mazure kitchen are different from the breakfast smells in the Walker kitchen. Instead of the smell of crispy fried bacon and golden fried eggs, aromas of coffee and buttery pastries greet him. The working class have smells, the ruling class aromas.

'Bonjour, bonjour ... good morning Hurtle are you early ... or am I late?' Léon Mazure's gruff morning voice matches his stocky build. His thick, dark moustache unfolds like a stage curtain beneath his nose, ending in rapier-like

wax tips over his cheeks. He has the look of the consummate Frenchman. But
the gruff voice is all a show. He smiles warmly and goes about pecking a
feisty 'bonjour' on the cheeks of his wife and children.

'Bonjour, Emil ...'

'Morning ... Dad ...'

'French please, Emil.'

'Bonjour, Papa ...'

'Emil ... I will speak English with Hurtle. You, mon petite garçon, will
speak French in the house ... it is the only way to learn.'

'Oui, Papa'

'Now ... Hurtle ... the chickens ...'

'Poulets ... papa ...'

'Yes, yes, Emil ... the chickens need to be fed. And a branch from the gum
tree came down last night; chop it for firewood. You will find the axe and
saw in the woodshed. Stack the wood inside the shed to dry. Oh ... and be
careful of ... ah ... le petit coq ...'

'Little rooster, Dad ...'

'Yes, Emil ... the little rooster, Hurtle.'

'Bantam ... Dad ...'

'Enough Emil ... the little bantam rooster Hurtle ... he has a temper ... does
he not Emil?'

'Oui papa ...'

∞

Léon Mazure's travels had taken him far from his home in Burgundy. His adventures and tales of other places would have made quite
an impression on a boy from the quiet village of Magill. To Hurtle
Walker the wider world was vast place of continents in the pages of an
atlas, as infinite and unreachable as outer space. Today our world is

small. Round the world air tickets can be purchased as easily as a bus ticket. And students from across the globe travel to Magill to study at university and experience cultural diversity. Léon Mazure was not only Hurtle's boss but also his mentor and guide at a pivotal time in his life. Léon Mazure was the means by which Hurtle Walker had access to the craftsmen, the knowledge, the tools and incentive that would show an unskilled boy the pathway to a better life. The French vignerons of Auldana taught Hurtle the craft of winemaking, and the fine art of *méthode champenoise*.

23

Méthode champenoise

I only drink champagne when I'm happy, and when I'm sad.
Sometimes I drink it when I'm alone.
When I have company, I consider it obligatory.
I trifle with it if I am not hungry and drink it when I am.
Otherwise I never touch it—unless I'm thirsty...

Lady Bollinger

In the stables behind a grand house on Home Park Estate, Hurtle
Walker learned the art of *méthode champenoise* from Léon Edmond

Mazure. Home Park Estate comprised the house, the stables and extensive vineyards. When Mazure bought the property from Patrick Auld he renamed the house *La Perouse*, after French explorer Jean Francois Galaup La Perouse, and the stables *La Perouse Cellars.* Mazure's La Perouse Cellars eventually found a new home on the north-east corner of The Parade and Penfold Road.[27] In time the cellars became Romalo Wines, where Hurtle and Norm Walker made superb sparkling wine.

The word champagne is an enigma as complex as the French word 'terroir'. Champagne, the word, does not transport my mind to a region in France. Instead it evokes images of celebration, fun, popping corks and beautiful, bubbling flutes caressed by beautiful bubbling women. Champagne is James Bond—sophistication, fashion, sex and starbursts of fireworks across a black sky. Champagne that is made beyond the boundaries of the Champagne region in France can no longer be referred to as Champagne. We must now call it 'Sparkling Wine'. The words sparkling wine, are what they are. No mystery or history there. It is wine that sparkles: pretty tame really.

Champagne is liquid fantasy and 'terroir' is the genie in the bottle: an unbeatable combination for entry into the happy-ever-after. Champagne brings with it much ado about drinking. Champagne is claimed to increase sexual desire—a liquid aphrodisiac that men eagerly pour for women at parties. So when my teenage daughter asked me where the bubbles in champagne come from, I told her that live yeast cells eat the sugar in the wine and fart the bubbles. As the wine ages the yeast cells die and split open, literally spilling their guts into the liquid and giving champagne its complex yeasty flavours. It worked—she will never touch the 'disgusting stuff'.

Stories abound and myths surround.

.e monk and cellarmaster, Dom Perignon, is credited
ınder' that brought the bubbling nectar into being. While
ıne for his brethren, around 1700, he supposedly com-
menι corking bottles of still wine before the fermentation process
was complete. The wine sat quietly in the cold dark cellars of the abbey
of Hautvillers, near the city of Reims, capital of the Champagne
region, throughout winter. But in the spring fermentation recom-
menced inside the sealed bottles through naturally occurring yeast.
The thin walls of still wine bottles are not designed to withstand
excessive pressure from the carbon dioxide trapped inside. They began
to explode. Dom rummaged around the cellar until he found one
bottle that was still intact. He upended the contents into his mouth
then cried out to his brothers, 'Come quickly! I am drinking stars.'[28]

The Dom Perignon account may or may not be entirely accurate,
but it doesn't matter. It is exactly the kind of emblematic story that
adds to the mystique and allure that surround champagne. Dom's
accidental discovery evolved over time to become the bottle fermentation method for the making of fine champagne, known today as
méthode champenoise.

Making exceptional champagne is labour-intensive and extremely
difficult. Mastery of *méthode champenoise* is achieved in specific phases.
The base wine must be a premium, still, dry white wine made from
carefully selected quality fruit. Discerning champagne makers use
Chardonnay and Pinot Noir grape varieties for the base wine. The
grapes are harvested (*vendange*) and the juice is extracted by a press
(*pressage*). Primary fermentation then commences as 'the key reaction
of winemaking is alcoholic fermentation, the conversion of sugar into
alcohol'.[29] Blending *La Cuvée* (*assemblage*) comes next; it is the selection
of the base wine from the mix of juices of the chosen grape varieties.

Chardonnay is a white grape with white juice (*blanc de blanc*). Pinot Noir is a red grape with *white* juice which can colour the wine the longer the white juice is in contact with the red skins. It can ultimately determine the colour of the champagne. And it is how the pink, in pink champagne, is achieved.

So, blending *La Cuvée* is a skill carefully considered by the wine-maker. Exacting measures of sugar, yeast and yeast nutrients are added to the base wine and the blend placed into thick-walled bottles (*tirage*) that are temporarily sealed with 'crown seal' caps. The *tirage* is placed in a cool cellar to begin secondary fermentation (*prise de mousse*) in slow time (two to five years), producing alcohol and carbon dioxide. The sealed bottles now contain bubbles and the toasty flavours of champagne, imparted by a colony of drunken yeasts whose short lives consisted of eating, multiplying and dying, much the same as the lives of those the champagne is made for. Yeasts enrich the wine with flavours and create a profusion of the beady bubbles of definitive champagne.

After fermentation in the bottles, heavy sediment gathers in the neck. The wine has been stacked below in the cool cellars for at least two years. The sediment is forced to the neck of the bottle by the use of shaking tables. The wine is shaken four times a day, two turns at a time, gently easing the sediment to the cork. The sediment is dis-gorged from the individual bottles by hand, and the bottles are then re-corked and stacked for a further three months before they are foiled, labelled and packed for delivery.

It is calculated that between 1919 and 1962, when he relinquished the task, Hurtle Walker 'shook the lees' or sediment of wine to the cork in 4,708,500[30] bottles, without a hint of repetitive strain injury. Shaking is done when the ageing phase is complete, on 'shaking' or 'riddling' tables (*le remuage*). This process was invented by one of the famous champagne widows, Barbe-Nicole Clicquot Ponsardin, who first cut holes in her own kitchen table.[31] The champagne bottles are placed upside down in the holes cut into the tables at an angle of 75 degrees. The shaker goes to the cellar four times a day to give each bottle a shake (which is a 1/8th turn), while the bottles remain upside down. The process manoeuvres the dead yeast cells into the neck of the bottle for disgorging. In Hurtle's time disgorging was a labour-intensive, skilful task performed by an extremely dexterous operator.

The disgorger at Romalo Wines was Hurtle Walker's brother, Norman. Norman would remove the metal clip (*agrafe*) and work the temporary cork loose with a disgorging tool, while hooking his fore-finger over the end of the cork to control its progress, as the gas pressure from inside the bottle forced the cork from the neck. The bubbles would rise and release the cork, washing the residue from the bottle. Today the necks of the bottles are frozen upside down in an ice-salt bath, moulding an ice plug of dead yeast cells. The seals are removed and the frozen plug exits under gas pressure from within the bottle.

Cloudless, crisp, twinkling champagne is now ready for the final phase. Liquor, base wine and cane sugar (*dosage*) is added to adjust the wine to the required taste, and to top up the bottle. Superior corks from Spain or Portugal are inserted, and wire clasps are fitted by the *muselière* (muzzle) machine to muzzle the wine until it is ready to spring forth and *bite*.

All that is left now is the tasting: *À votre santé!*[32]

Edmond Mazure Champagne

Winemaker: Norm Walker

Colour: Pale and clear with a fine, very persistent bead

Nose: Shows distinct yeast (due to the very long period on lees) and genuine French Champagne character. This is further enhanced by the mature Pinot Noir varietal influence.

Palate: The palate is very soft, but crisp and refreshing. It is an elegant champagne by all standards, an outstanding wine.[33]

Unlike Dom Perignon, Hurtle Walker never made champagne by accident. But the stories that accompany his lifetime as a champagne maker have a similar emblematic magnetism.

During the Second World War American troops often came to Magill to buy their sparkling wines. One colonel drove his jeep to the golf course, some miles from Romalo Wines, one Sunday morning to persuade Hurtle to come back to the cellars so he could buy the cases of the sparkling wines the Americans were so fond of. The plane that was to take the troops back to their base in the Pacific Islands was so heavily laden with champagne it could scarcely rise above sea level, so they opened the bomb-bay doors and jettisoned some of the cases over the Adelaide foothills suburb of Mitcham.[34] This enabled the plane to gain enough altitude to clear the Mount Lofty Ranges. People living in the area woke to find cases of champagne in their gardens, mostly broken of course, but a few remained intact.

On another occasion Hurtle Walker was surprised to find a man waiting in his office with a medical prescription for tonic wine. A friend and fellow duck shooter, Dr Borthwick, sent the man to seek out Hurtle and ask him to suggest a tonic wine for the man's wife. Sparkling Burgundy was selected as the elixir to cure all ills. The dose was one glass at ten in the morning another at four in the afternoon, and the remainder of the bottle to be taken before going to bed. The man left with two dozen bottles. Two years later he returned to Romalo to seek-out Hurtle Walker once again, only this time to throttle him. As fate and perhaps the Sparkling Burgundy would have it, the man's wife gave birth to twins and the husband blamed both the wine and Hurtle. In the end he had to admit his wife's health and outlook on life had vastly improved. He left, happily toting another case of the tonic he continued to purchase for many years to come.[35]

Many such anecdotes chart the life of Hurtle Walker, winemaker.

In later years Hurtle Walker developed what was referred to as 'chalky gout', lumps as hard as walnuts on his knuckles and fingers. The gout disfigured one of his fingers so badly that he gouged divots from the greens each time he played competition bowls with the Kensington Gardens club. So he had the offending digit surgically removed to improve his follow-through.

'Grand-pop' Hurtle was once given the task of looking after the grandchildren up at the cellars, while mum Norma went into the city to do some shopping. When she got back the two youngest had newly acquired, perfectly shaped pacifiers in the form of champagne corks.

Hurtle and Norm Walker made world-class sparkling wines. Hurtle learned his craft the way it had been taught for centuries, passed on by those who had gone before. Norm Walker was qualified in the science of oenology. But he also had his father's guidance and knowledge to draw upon: the intuitive skills of the artisan that cannot be taught by science. Norm had the best of both worlds, but he always made a point of not wearing his lab coat when dad was around.

24

In the unlikely event of an emergency

The nauseating nasal tones of the female announcer override the screeching buzz that is also coming out of the radio. *Something must be wrong with the bastard thing.* Deep sleep has eluded me all night long and now somewhere far into the darkness the torturous noise of the alarm has finally put an end to the trying. I curse myself for not booking the flight for the afternoon. I hate waking up tired. I drag what feels like a one-hundred-year-old body out of bed while my wife becomes a doona sausage with relish.

Flash drive ... inside pocket of jacket ... papers ... under flap on the side of the small suitcase ... mints, cash, plastic cards, boarding pass, socks, jocks, shaving gear, shampoo ... oh my god SHAMPOO!

'You can't take the shampoo.'
'Why?'
'We need it.'
'Well so do I. You take it when you go away.'
'I take another bottle. You are taking the *only* bottle.'

'Why is there only ever another bottle when you go away?'

'It's too early in the morning for this.'

'Here, take the bloody thing, I don't want it.'

She begins looking through the cupboards.

'No, don't bother, I don't want any. I'll use soap. That's all I deserve. I mean who cares if more hairs fall out of my head ... nobody notices old farts like me anyway so why the hell does shampoo matter—keep the shampoo.'

'You're nervous aren't you?'

'Yes.'

∞

An orange mist washes the black sky above the stark neon glow of the terminal. *Do they have to use the word terminal?* I make my way past the throng of passengers roped into the cattle stalls and get an immediate call-up to the online check-in.

'Are you able and prepared to help the cabin crew in the unlikely event of an emergency?'

It's happened again. This is the third time in three flights I have been offered the privilege of more leg room in exchange for making calm and calculated judgements, under extreme duress, of the environmental and safety conditions outside of a Virgin airbus 'In the unlikely event of an emergency'. I must have that 'no longer a virgin to emergency exit procedures' look, or what must look like the legs of a giraffe.

On the previous occasion the cabin attendant who delivered the emergency exit speech was a young woman. I remember her leaning forward in a conspiratorial manner, the voice low and raspy, her dazzling eyes falling on the three of us men in the stretch limo seats. I don't know how much of what she said we actually took in, but we listened dutifully as our lanky outstretched limbs relaxed. I had the 'doggie in the window seat' at the time, and my job, she explained, 'in the unlikely event of an emergency,' was to peer through the face-sized porthole, do a quick survey of structural damage, and then assess any dangerous obstacles that may prevent passengers disembarking in a hurry.

To me structural damage and dangerous obstacles were missing wings, fire, sharks circling, terrorists waiting in gunships, and high water levels, or no water levels if we crashed on land. If I gave the 'all clear' then the cabin crew would order the passengers to prepare to leave the aircraft on my say-so. I would then pull down on the lever above the door, lift the door bodily into the cabin then hurl it like a discus from the hand of Hercules through the opening, paying attention to where it lands in case I need to reunite and cling to it later. The two men beside me gave me a 'good luck with that then mate' look.

'Well?' repeats the girl at the check-in, 'Can you help?' Her doe-like eyelashes flutter, but her eyes challenge me—*Well, can you? Can you do it? Do you have it in you, daddy long legs?* I return the look with steely determination and flutter my own eyelashes back at her. 'If I can stop screaming long enough I will.' She doesn't get the humour and finds me another seat at the back of the plane.

∞

I am off to a biography conference in Canberra.

The last time I spoke with Norm Walker to tell him I was going to Canberra, he shocked me with the story that his dad's war medals were missing. Norm had received a letter the previous year from the Australian War Memorial, asking to borrow the medals for a special display commemorating Hurtle Walker's old battalion. Norm sent the medals up, but they never came back. So I promised I would do some digging while I was there.

The pass through security is painless: a nervous toilet break and then on to gate 16 to await the call. Even though I have been allocated a seat, I really would like to sit up front with the captain. So I can keep an eye on what he is doing. We board, and I squeeze myself into a window seat. My knees are now supporting my chin and I regret not gratefully accepting the offer of more leg room.

The carry-on luggage passengers are creating a problem. Bulging bags the size of small coffins are being cursed and wrestled into tiny crevices in the overhead lockers. It looks likely the emergency inflatable dingy will be sacrificed to accommodate the bags. I can hear a revised instruction, "in the unlikely event of an emergency please remove your coffins and climb inside."

We are finally underway. Babies cry as their ears begin to pop and passengers like me grip armrests as we taxi for so long to the runway we could be driving to Canberra. The commodore of cabin attendants puts on his best Barry White vocal and caresses us with deep, resonant, breathy tones through the cabin speakers. 'We are about to dim the lights and get romantic ... take the hand of the person next to you and spread the love ... spread the love ... yeah ... try a little kiss ... yeah.' Giggles and embarrassed looks turn to laughter as the rich Barry tones are suddenly replaced by a squeaky 'Whoa! The front row's really goin' for it!'

The street lights of Adelaide are now far beneath us and the nerves have gone. Well done commodore.

∞

The conference is especially good. My paper causes a little controversy but is enthusiastically received, and the drinks and nibbles are superb. It is day three and I decide to skip the afternoon session to find the War Memorial and look for Hurtle's medals.

I walk around the biggest lake in Canberra. The long, wrong way round, as it turns out, wearing leather boots that are much too tight. It is a hot day. I trek the continuous incline of the striking red gravel road that heralds the entrance to the War Memorial. The boots pinch at the softest contours of my feet and the relentless blowflies bathe in the salty pools of perspiration in the corners of my eyes.

I curse out loud with every step then chide myself for my soft, self-pity as I pass monuments to soldiers who had travelled the roads and trails of unimaginable struggles. I too have a mission.

I think of Hurtle Walker and his battles in the Somme mud. I think of Norm Walker, who regretted not talking to his father about the war. Now the medals were missing and I was their only hope. I lift my eyes and look at the memorial. It sits in monolithic pose in the folds of the hillside, a stone sentinel wrapped protectively around its charges. Without conscious effort, I square my shoulders, straighten my back, and climb the steps. I enter the great cavern where I immediately become overwhelmed by the emotion in the air around me: the breath of the living seeking the dead.

After a long and arduous game of bureaucratic musical chairs, blather and buck-passing along with an offer of an officially written apology, I sadly concede I will not be going home with Hurtle's medals.

∞

'Norm, there was not a lot I could do. There's an unbelievable amount of stuff stored in the bowels of that building. The medals could be anywhere. I know it's no comfort, but they offered a written apology.'

I decided to tell him the bad news on arriving home. He is in bed resting his knee, which has been causing him a lot of pain lately. But this look of pain has nothing to do with the knee. He points over my shoulder. 'Could you have a bit of a look in that cupboard, at the back of the top drawer?' The drawer is filled with socks and jocks. I plunge my hand deep into a cotton labyrinth of Bonds briefs and rummage my way to the back. My fingers find a flat box.

Hurtle's medals were in Norm's sock drawer the whole time.

25

The boys of war

Let the boy try along this bayonet-blade
How cold steel is, and keen with hunger of blood;
Blue with all malice, like a madman's flash;
And thinly drawn with famishing for flesh.
Lend him to stroke these blind, blunt bullet heads
Which long to muzzle in the hearts of lads,
Or give him cartridges of fine zinc teeth,
Sharp with the sharpness of grief and death.
For his teeth seem for laughing round an apple.
There lurk no claws behind his fingers supple;
And God will grow no talons at his heels,
Nor antlers through the thickness of his curls.[36]

The Wilfred Owen poem *Arms and the Boy* should have been part of the text on every recruitment poster for the Great War, World War One. But it was written too late for a war that began in absurdity and ended in great tragedy.

If we know anything about the 1914–1918 war it is how young the soldiers were. The young boys and young men with castles in the air, dreams of adventure that would pluck them from the mundane routines of everyday life, take them across the globe, and introduce them to the terrible routines of everyday death. The boys of war could not have imagined the horrors that awaited them.

In conversations about World War One there is always somebody's grandfather or great-uncle who fudged their age so they could go and do their duty. Out of the ten 'boys in the vines' photo only four survived the war: one outrageous statistic from one small village in faraway Magill. And many others never made it back to Magill. My great-grandmother blew the whistle on my own grandfather, who was sent home when it was discovered he was just fourteen years and eight months old: the youngest despatch rider in the Royal Irish Fusiliers. He was one of the lucky ones. I can see great-granny McDonald wrestling with young Henry as she drags him home by the ear.

Having older men in the ranks helped balance the ledger. Boy soldiers looked to the men for assurance and confidence and drew strength from their presence.

One such man was Hurtle Walker.

Hurtle was a man of 24 when he enlisted 'as a private in the Australian Imperial Force on 7 September 1915.'[37] Fanciful boyhood notions of adventures in war would not have been a defining reason for Hurtle to join up. He lived an idyllic existence in idyllic surroundings and his everyday life was far from mundane. He was a valuable and skilled winemaker working at the Auldana winery at a time when local manpower and boy power was severely depleted by the call-up. He had a strong sense of loyalty to his employer, but his sense of duty in the decision to serve his country clearly had the greater pull.

Hurtle was going to war, and Jarrah got excited.
He left Melbourne for Egypt on 5 January 1916 with the 2nd Reinforcements for the 6th Field Artillery Brigade. On St Patrick's Day he

embarked at Alexandria on the *Ibo* with 500 horses, bound for Marseilles. The troops boarded a train to Le Havre where they spent three days in tents in the snow. From Le Havre it was on to Armentières and then Fleur Bay.[38] Hurtle Walker was seeing much of a world he had only ever heard about. He had never ventured far from Magill. But now he had crossed the oceans by ship to Egypt and France. He experienced snow, which never fell on Magill. He was in Léon Edmond Mazure's homeland, and soon he would be tested in battle. Hurtle joined the 6th Brigade at Belloy-sur-Somme on 19July 1916.

The energetic, athletic boy from the place called Magill became a leader of men and a hero on the battlefields of France. 'His courage and stamina in handling horses, limbers and heavy ordnance amid carnage earned him the Distinguished Conduct Medal (DCM) and the Military Medal and Bar'. The unit diary declares him 'the most decorated non-commissioned officer of the Brigade'. Hurtle was promoted in the field to sergeant and finished his service as a warrant officer class 2 (WO2).[39]

When Norm Walker was a young boy, he read his father's war diaries. He read about the gas canisters and explosives that fell from Zeppelins in the night sky. He read about the unbearable cold and the soul-sucking mud. The diaries are long gone, lost, along with the insights of a father at war. A diary is a private place to unburden the soul of inner feelings that an official story doesn't tell.

Soldiers go to war with an army, but they fight the war alone.

Norm always believed that Hurtle was an inspiration to the boy soldiers in his unit. Hurtle was gassed and wounded in battle during three separate encounters. His bravery was extraordinary and it came with the highest of accolades.

The 'Bar to Military Medal' citation below reads:

'At 5.20.pm on the 18th of September 1918 near LE VER-GUIER's (*sic*) a sudden and heavy bombardment with instantaneous fuze (*sic*) and gas shell was put down close to the battery position. The first shells landed right beside the teams of R.F.A. wagons in a valley to the right of the battery. Four horses of one team were wounded or killed and the driver pinned beneath the struggling animals. Sergeant WALKER rushed through the heavy fire to the team and under a constant hail of shells and flying splinters extricated the driver who subsequently died of his wounds. He then released the remaining horse which he succeeded in freeing but the bombardment was so heavy that the horse was killed before it had gone 30 yards. He displayed bravery of the highest order under the heaviest fire and his fine example had an excellent effort on the personnel. He was awarded the D.C.M in June 1917 and the Military Medal in November 1917.'[40]

(Sgd) WALTER A. COHEN. Brig. Gen.

I read extracts from the *London Gazette* with amazement and wonder. Passages lift the spirit in admiration: 'The pit caught fire and ammunition began to explode. Walker, without hesitation, entered the burning pit and assisted the wounded to a place of safety.' My mind wants to re-enact the scene to feel a sense of what he was going through, but it can't. Flashes of fire and chaos and noise and the cracking thumps of exploding shells are only a spectator's view. In the pit he felt the scorching heat and heard the screams of the wounded. The cracking thumps of exploding ammunition would have shocked his senses and shaken his resolve. But those who endure win. With over 4,000 rounds exploding in the hellfire that surrounded him, Hurtle Walker continued to assist the wounded to safety, and when the infantry called for retaliation to hostile fire, 'Walker going into pit No.3 worked the gun by himself.'[41]

It takes a rare individual, with unshakeable presence of mind and monumental self-control, to cope in such horrific situations. Hurtle Walker was one such individual. During the whole of the war only seven Australians were awarded the DCM, MM and bar out of a total of 300,000 troops. His devotion to his fellow man was exemplary. Hurtle Walker sits in the Pantheon of unique Australian heroes.

By all accounts Hurtle and Norm Walker are very much alike: humorous, generous, hospitable and kind. They both enjoyed sports and the manly pursuits of hunting and fishing. Norm's life-path mirrored his father's in the wine industry and neither of them wanted to live anywhere but Magill. I've seen pictures of Hurtle Walker in later life with his grandchildren; he has the warm and loving face of a proud grandfather.

Norm Walker remembers his father as a man who never raised his hand or his voice to his children. They never had a disagreement the whole time they worked together at Romalo. Hurtle Walker was the kind of man who never forced his will on anybody, and always had a kind word for those around him.

He was a gentle man. How could such a man be so formidable a soldier? Hurtle would not have regarded himself a hero. He was *Jarrah*—strong, resilient and true. True to those who needed his strength. True to the boys and the men and the horses that were his unit. His duty was of a higher calibre. His duty saved lives.

Hurtle came home from the clatter of the guns and the chaos of war to the wines he left waiting for his return, maturing silently in slow time in the cool dark cellars of Magill. On 26 July 1923 Hurtle married Ellen Eliza 'Nellie' Grattan, a country girl from Elliston on South Australia's far west coast. Together they built their home amid the vines, put down their roots in Magill and started a family. Joyce Hamp Walker was born on 16 February 1925, and Norman John, 'Norm,' Walker on 18 March 1929.[42]

26

Monuments

It's a bright autumn morning and I feel the urge to wander. I pack a rucksack with sandwiches, a bottle of water, notepad and pen, and head out the back door. Autumn days in Magill glisten and glitter under intense blue skies.

It is Mediterranean weather and by far the best season of the South Australian climate. I will mount 'shank's pony'[43] and roam wherever the day will take me.

I look across the street. Norm has more than enough leaves to keep him busy. He sweeps; they fall. He sweeps; they fall. Across Penfold Road a whining chainsaw is having a relentless argument with some firewood, and on Penfold Road everybody's got a brrumm … brrumm. I turn east up Ormond Avenue away from the noise, the traffic and the 'pacers' who have just been let loose to assault the pavements. Today is a day for strolling.

It's only when I feel the warmth of the sun on my face that I realise I forgot the sunscreen, the hat and the long sleeves. All the annoying extras the experts harp incessantly about in their lofty quest to protect the ignorant from themselves. I return to the house and start again.

Walk with me a while.

At the top of the street we turn into Young Park, a shaded grove of dark, slender trees that lean at peculiar angles to the ground. The copse connects Ormond Avenue to Romalo Avenue in a quaint walk-through. The land was donated by the parents of Cynthia E 'Bunty' Bonython, who lives in gracious Romalo House nearby. Romalo House was once Home Park and La Perouse where Hurtle Walker and Léon Edmond Mazure made champagne in the stables. The name Romalo combines the names 'Roma' and 'Lois,' daughters of two directors of Romalo Wines. Large wrought-iron gates front the entrance to Romalo House.

The original gates once stood on Penfold Road at a time when Romalo Avenue was the private roadway to the stately home.

Thelma Schubert lives at 13 Romalo Avenue. Early Marcher, Craig Rossiter, lives at number 11 and John Dillon once lived at number 31. Thelma is the wife of Grange Hermitage architect, Max Schubert. Craig Rossiter is Thelma's supportive neighbour and Norm Walker's friend. John Dillon played golf with Max Schubert. And John's son is a friend of the parents of my son's school friend. From this one street, intersecting threads of meaning spread out across Magill. That is what a neighbourhood is. People who know people who know people.

Enough talk, let's walk.

We cross Romalo and slide down Elm into Giles Street. Giles Street is very much alive with self-employed gardeners lost in an orchestral score of whipping and snipping and grinding and blowing. Up Giles Street to Burchett and down into Adelaide Street.

On Adelaide Street the Magill School stands proud, looking splendid in its modern makeover: not just a facelift, but new buildings, new equipment, new decor and new determination and enthusiasm for the twenty-first century. If a school could strut, I think this one would.

A right turn onto Penfold Road takes us downhill to the hub of the village where we will cross at the intersection and walk along St Bernard's Road to the university.

The faces, shapes and colours of the inhabitants on the streets of Magill are as diverse as the wider world. The newcomers are from Asia, India, Africa, Indonesia and Malaysia. When they appear in the streets it startles you: like finding strawberries in the forest: black Africa, alabaster Asia and variegated India. He wears a majestic white turban, flowing white robes, his hair and beard are startling against his coffee-coloured skin. She walks serenely behind him swathed in green silk, a vivid red dot on her forehead.

Old-comers came from the British Isles, Ireland, Italy, Greece, Yugoslavia and Germany. Newcomers come for a better life. Old-comers came for the same reason. Newcomers bring exotic foods, exotic clothes and cultural traditions that are changing the aesthetic face of Magill and its surrounds. They also bring a level of disquiet to the old-comers. Old-comers watch them establish businesses and fill the churches they once filled. And they ponder over some of the new-comers' fine homes and expensive cars. To some old-comers it seems the newcomers brought the better life with them. Old-comers forged the foundations: the early struggles, the buildings, the commerce, sacrifices in war, and the monuments. The monuments that lay claim and bear testament to the establishment of place.

The soft Scottish brogue of a woman at a party, on the previous Saturday night, echoes in my head and draws me out of my reverie. She said we should do more about our heritage because, as she pointed out, 'we have so little of it.'

But the streets of Magill are paved with our heritage and the vines on the hillsides are laden with it. You only need to look.

Long strides take me down deep brick steps, past towering Cypress trees planted with seeds brought from Rome in 1910. I cross Third Creek on the narrow footbridge and walk across the campus grounds to Murray House.

Murray House stands like a fortress above the grounds of the university: a bedrock testament to heritage and permanence and settle-ment, and a tribute to the skills of the craftsmen who built it. Many rooms behind many doors are set in distinctive bluestone walls: rooms in the high tower, rooms with windows shaded by shutters, rooms sheltered under lattice-trimmed verandahs, rooms of establishment and order and change. A powerful image from the landscape of an old world nestled comfortably in the landscape of the new.

I meet up with a student and together we admire Murray House. I ask her if she believes the stories of a place live with its monuments.

She doesn't notice or think about buildings or monuments. 'Most young people don't connect with things that don't refer to them or concern them personally'.

We sit and talk.

Jess is an Australian-born student with Vietnamese and Chinese parents. Her impressions of Magill are based on casual everyday observations. She sees Magill as very Australian and 'olden days.'

We talk about her generation. She is generation 'Y'[44] and she believes her generation is judged unfairly. She admits she is too reliant on technology. 'I couldn't access money for lunch yesterday because I left my mobile phone at home,' she laughs.

I ask her what she thinks of the elderly: 'It's the time of generation Y, and generation X[45]—we are the future. We tend to disregard things past. Old people have had their time.'

Jess believes some cultures treat their elderly better than others. Asian cultures 'adhere to respect, but there is also a grain of fear.' Her Asian boyfriend reveres his grandparents and he is 'kind and gentle with them.' But Jess thinks the nice older person is a 'stereotype that doesn't always hold up.'

She tells me that an Asian background is both a blessing and a curse. 'While Asian children are thoroughly looked after, nagging is regularly used as a primary tool to instil guilt. And there is an overwhelming pressure to look after our parents as they grow old.'

∞

Over St Bernard's Road the Interpretative Walk[46] beckons. I stretch my legs along the banks of Third Creek and stop to look at the cluster of storyboards—a public memory to the past. I can't help but wonder if that past will end with generation Y.

In 1842 there were around 650 Aborigines in Adelaide and surrounding districts. By 1852 the population had reduced to about 180. The etchings describe how the clearing of the forests, the shooting of the birds and wildlife and the diseases that came with the settlers devastated the indigenous population. By 1855, the indigenous people had moved deeper into the foothills. The irony in the tale is that the voice of the dispossessed is represented by the recollections of a settler named Lillywhite.

Truth is in the imagination.[47]

The Kaurna people lived by the creeks that meandered through a forest of giant gum trees. The monoliths protected and fed them, body and soul. In their stories of the Dreamtime,[48] sprits of dead ancestors were white. So the bewildering appearance of the early white settlers must have baffled and frightened them. They believed the white men were the ghosts of their own dead. Indigenous spirits had 'sinew eye' or 'lightning eye' and to look into the eye of a spirit meant a flash of certain death.[49] These white spirits spat the lightning flash of certain death from sticks they held to their eye. These white spirits could pluck birds from the sky and animals from the land; they had tools that decimated the forest and beasts that took the trees away.

Standing in the modern, neatly trimmed landscape of Nightingale Reserve with its tennis courts, children's playground and scout hall, the past still rustles with the wind in the trees. It is all still here in the earth beneath my feet and in the air around me. Here, where Norm Walker's great-grandfather built a shanty to shelter his family. Here, where the last major battle fought between the Kaurna and the Peramangk[50] people took place.

I look to the distant past.

Women and children stand behind the battle lines. They would be close to their husbands and fathers if the unspeakable happened. The Kaurna line is compact: each man a column in the wall with Wokali shields held close to their chests.

The Hills tribe breaks its line again and again as individuals run forward with high-pitched wails, and insults to rile and intimidate the Kaurna. The numbers on both sides surge as long jagged spears mock the air. One voice from the Kaurna line is heard clearly above the rest. The Hills tribe quickly reforms. In a terrible silence two volleys of long spears slash the sunlight. The deadly arc is precise. Barbed shafts hover at the pinnacle momentarily, in a connecting arc. The eyes of each man are wide and alert to the shape of his fate. Tips coil downwards as the long sticks snake in descent; quivering and humming they drop from the sky. In one stark moment a brittle clatter resounds as each spear is taken by a shield. Sharp tips split the pipe-clay coating and probe the bark protector as blood and ochre merge across the surface[51](*Neill 2010*).

I leave the ghosts and the warriors and the echoes of battle behind, and make my way downhill to St George's Church.

∞

Eerie silence stalks me as I enter the church grounds. There is no-one around. No traffic. No sound. Far from today's world I stand in a place where those whose images I've seen in timeworn books, lie close to their totem. Close to their elaborate cairn, to their holy place, their monument of faith and existence. One-by-one they brought the stones from the creek nearby. One-by-one they brought the stones to build their church: One-by-one.

In a cavity beneath the church's foundation stone a glass jar was discovered. It contained silver coins from the 1840s, and the remnants of a document which read:

> May this sacred edifice, which is to be raised by the voluntary exertion of the inhabitants of Woodforde and its vicinity, serve as a memorial to their anxiety to secure for themselves and their posterity the ordinances of religion, as also of their attachment to the church of their fathers.[52]

Burial grounds tend to unnerve me. I step carefully amongst the orderly rows in the cemetery. The narrow spaces between the graves are tricky. I leap over some, tiptoe round and then long-stride over others, to avoid stepping on them. *I hope no-one is watching.* A grave, as opposed to an urn full of ashes, makes me feel the person is still here. Some of the graves have simple crosses etched with a name and a date. Others have ornately chiselled headstones that tell the story of a life. I read the words on the headstone of one unusually small grave that is set apart from the rest ... *Christopher Rawson Penfold died April 27 1870.*

Contemplation gives way to sadness.

A weather-beaten teddy lies face down near the headstone of a boy who lived for two weeks.

I read the words written for a 17-year-old girl in 1872. *Her memory breathes a sweetness that survives her living days.* I come to a shaded patch on the dusty path where small white flowers grow in ever-widening circles. There is no reasonable explanation for this concentric floral display growing in the middle of the walkway. Perhaps artistic self-pollination took place from flowers nearby. I desperately want to count the delicate flowers. But I dare not. In case they match the number of graves.

Enough now, leave them be.

I leave beneath the roof of the lych-gate.[53]And walk back up the hill
to the Tower Hotel. The Tower was once known as the Woodforde
Arms and the East Torrens Hotel. With its ornate iron-lace balcony
and landmark high tower, it owes its early beginnings to the work of
Captain Thomas Brooks Penfold, who built the first structure on the
site in 1852.[54] Many changes have taken place over the years. Today,
gaming machines are almost a licence to print money for the hotel
industry. Multi-million dollar modern extensions and renovations of
old South Australian pubs are now commonplace. The changes sit well
on some, whereas on others they are a parasitic intrusion. But the
Tower got it right. It wears its modern self well. At the front it
proudly displays its past to the present, and at the back the present is
embedded in its past. The hotel is just as inviting to the thirsty traveller as it ever was.

Magill was a crossroads for travellers venturing to settle the vast
open spaces inland. The Tower and the World's End Inn met their
every need. The hurricane lamps that glowed through the darkness
outside the old hotels were a welcome sight to weary travellers. The
settlers, the coach builders, the farmers and the World's End Inn, are
now distant memories. But memories of the enduring monuments of
Magill are stories waiting to be told.

∞

My pony is tired. I amble along Penfold Road as an Indian man in a
peak cap strolls toward me. Three small, unleashed dogs are on his
right side, blocking the passing space. The man tips his cap, smiles at
me, and says, in what could only be described as a Londoner's cockney
accent …'aft' noon sir, keep to the left please.'

I am now in a culturally confused time warp with a hat-tipper and his three dogs.

I take my pony home.

27

Memory place

Small white and yellow blooms flourish at the base of the verandah wall where Nellie used to sit and watch for the rare sight of a passing car on Penfold Road. At the side of the house, a cluster of pink lilies on a single stalk appears without fail each year and long-stem vivid red flowers grow from gaps in the foundations around the house. I never planted any of them. The flowers are from another time, another garden. I like to think it was Nellie's garden: the past existing in the present.

I walk around the house. It desperately needs work. The green gables are peeling and dry rot can be seen at the ends of each barge board. Salt damp is making its way up the bricks on one side wall and part of the sandy foundation is crumbling on the other. The brush fence is sagging and ragged and ready to surrender to gravity. Our Beagle, Pip, sits on top of a verandah pillar next to the spot where Nellie sat. He licks my ear as I walk by. Pip is on guard. From his high vantage point he scans Penfold Road, ready to howl into action at the first sign of a gigantic lycra-pede on wheels. Lycra-clad 'cycle bots' pass the house in droves every day. It would have pleased Hurtle Walker; he excelled as a competitive cyclist. But I'm not sure what he would have thought of lycra.

I look up beneath the verandah roof. Networks of spider webs high up in the rafters make me shudder. Huntsman spiders pop up everywhere—on the windows of the car or on a light switch in the dark; one even clung to the side of my coffee cup as I put it to my mouth, early one morning. Ugly black spiders are always lurking, ready to scuttle out of a corner and across a room, sending the family squealing in the opposite direction. Spiders are a common sight about the house. Despite the assurance that 'they're good for the garden' they insist on coming inside. And no matter how much spraying, squealing and escorting them outside, usually on the bristle end of a long-handled broom, takes place, we still shake our shoes in the mornings and conduct sun visor and air vent checks whenever we use the cars. 'It's because you live so close to the vineyards,' it was suggested over dinner one evening. 'Plant some lavender *darling*.'

Old houses should have cobwebs anyway.

A broken pane by the front door evokes memories of other broken windows. The whole house is a memory place. I go inside. I will always see the 'lady in the garden' each time I am in the passage and the light falls across the wall in a certain way. I see my children as babies again and hear the songs I sang to them each time I pass their rooms. And whenever I am in the family room, I re-live the celebrations we had there again and again, and feel the tears of joy and sadness that life brings into a home. I will always remember the man who built the house and his son who still comes to visit. And at night, when the gully breezes sweep down from the hills, I will remember the storm that battered the house that Hurtle built.

Let me recall it for you.

It was a two-peg night. The garage door was blowing off its hinges. In the dark, wee small hours we were going to have to get out of bed and fix it.

It was at the end of a period of extreme heat. Twelve days of over 40 degrees Celsius culminated in high winds that broke lamps, tore the lid off the barbecue and sent it crashing into a window, tossed watering cans to set them rolling and tumbling into the garden, stripped branches from trees and toppled shrubs in pots about the yard. The wind doubled in velocity as we entered the garage, sending spades, shovels and rakes chasing after us. The front door billowed like a mainsail in full flight.

In bra and knickers and jocks and socks we wrestled the door into position and banged home two large tent pegs at its base. With the front door secure the wind was now trying to push the rear door into the garage. We struggled to slide the door into place. But we were being lifted by the roots of our hair by an invisible, coiled demon that had turned a gully breeze into a gully gale. We pushed and pulled. My groin began to quiver. I was about to let go of the door when rage and the fear of being hit by an airborne Weber helped us drag it, screeching along its unoiled rails and slot it home.

Back in the house, the children, the dogs and the birds were all sound asleep, wrapped securely within four walls.

The house has stood for ninety years. It could stand for ninety more. And for as long as it does all the memories will linger.

28

Algonquin round table

Early Marchers! You are cordially invited to attend a 'gathering of the tribe' on Wednesday June 19 at 1:30 pm in Norm's Snooker Room. Finger food and nibbles will be provided to sweeten the pot. You are most welcome to bring liquid refreshment of your own choosing.

Norm Walker

He looks at the platter.

'What are *they*?'
'Chivapchichis'
'Eh?'
'Also, *polskie orgorkie* dill pickles, Kalamatta olives, Jarlsberg, goat, ambrosia, and some other cheeses: smoked trout pâté, crackers and mini toasts.'
'Jesus!'
'What did *you* get?'
'Little pies, pasties, sausage rolls and a bottle of tomato sauce.'
'Well we've got it covered then, Norm.'

I can tell he is nervous.

They arrive earlier than expected. We arrange the chairs in a closed circle at one end of the snooker table. It will be our 'Algonquin round table'.[55] All will be seated, seen and heard. The snooker table is covered with a yellow vinyl sheet. In the centre is the platter. Surrounded by strategically placed nibbles; in case my wife's lovingly prepared delicacies look too strange to visit.

I have met some Early Marchers before: Max Cooper, Craig Rossiter, Max Ramsay and Jamie Shepherd. The rest don't look familiar to me. Craig, Jamie Norm and I are the only Magillians in the room.

George Collet is new to me. He is a slight man with an agreeable way about him. His Early Marchers' name is 'Bosun'. George put the group together in 1966. They were all around the age of 40 then: too old to be members of Apex and too young to retire to easy chairs. George has dementia. He sits quietly alongside Max Cooper, who is looking out for him. In the beginning it was George's shack at Port Willunga[56] (Port Willy) that hosted the main event each year. Early in the month of March was the time for dirty deeds or harmless fun … whichever was on the menu.

I notice that the food on the platter is disappearing fast. Red wine is flowing freely and Norm has gone to get the pies and pasties from the oven in the house. Close conversations are taking place and old photographs, spread across one end of the pool table, are being ignored.

Norm returns with the pies, pasties and Rosella tomato sauce. 'It's as cold as charity in here,' he says. 'Shall I turn the heater on?' The room howls him down. 'The red will keep us warm, Norm.'

After some years at Port Willy, George suggested going somewhere else.

Who could blame him? He probably wanted to keep what was left of his beach shack intact. George had done the research. He had somewhere more adventurous in mind. Somewhere like Innamincka. The idea suited Coop. Innamincka was on Cooper's Creek. It gave him a degree of kinship with the place.

They were organised. Written invitations delegated responsibilities. Cultural Pursuits: sightseeing and magazines. Transport Officer: vehicles and storage. Fishing and Boats: tackle, bait, tinnies[57] and fuel. Sports: shooting, cribbage, beach cricket, and nude bathing. *Or was that beach bathing and nude cricket?*

Innamincka was the seminal trip away, early in March of 1975. It forged a doctrine for the future and gave birth to the Early Marchers' heart stone: the Innamincka Ice Box.

Max Cooper cooked the first meal: a barbecue on the banks of Cooper's Creek. There is dissent over what species of fish was cooked, Yellow Belly or Barramundi. More importantly, the group want an explanation from Coop they have waited 35 years to hear. They want to know why he dumped their entire supply of cutlery into Cooper's Creek. He arches his eyebrows, and with a puzzled look shrugs his shoulders. George grins.

Norm remembers large, sinister-looking crows circling the sky above their camp. When the Early Marchers went sightseeing, the crows rampaged through the campsite like terrorists, scattering shotgun shells and cans of Cooper's Big Barrel Beer. Stories and jibes flood the room as memories are dusted and oiled.

Coop: 'You got your hearing aid turned on, Norm?'
Norm: 'What? ...yeah.'
Coop: 'Get your money back.'

They discuss old friends who are no longer with them: Harry the Horse, Davey Jefferies (Winsey) and David Burchell (Hoppy). Craig Rossiter keeps them on track with dates and names.

Jamie and Norm relive a trip to Donovan's Landing, near Nelson, a town over-the-border in Victoria. Out for his morning jog, Jamie discovered a group of cricketers preparing for a match against long-established South Australian rivals. 'They were a motley crew,' explains Norm, who played competitive sport all his life. They were not overly concerned with fitness. They smoked while fielding, dropped the cigarette when the ball came close, then picked the butts back up 'for another puff' once they had fielded the ball. Running singles was a no-no. This socially-driven, raggedy bunch hit fours and sixes so they would not have to run at all.

It's hard to keep up. Some stories begin and have no end. Others are contested for accuracy. It has become the floor of parliament as interjections and cries of 'Mr Speaker! Mr Speaker!' zing back and forth across the room. There is much laughter and affirmation of brotherhood. The pantomime brings back their shared past. 'I strenuously object, Mr Speaker, it wasn't Port Willy it was ...'

Time has caught up with them. They are older now but the same in spirit as I imagine they always were: the same moderators, the same storytellers, the same dissenters. George sits quietly with a look of wonder behind his soft smile. He was their leader. Now, he is the focus of their attention and concern. He is with Coop, and Coop is holding on tight.

I begin to see the value in the nicknames. They are used in place of real names when the stories get too close for comfort. *That wasn't me that was somebody called Medic and Medic is an Early Marcher, an alter-ego, an alias to protect the guilty.* Some nicknames have shady origins, and others are eloquent when paired ... Mulga Mick and Desert Trek Dick.

Their adventures always took them close to water.

In a sheltered cove near Venus Bay, on the far west coast of South Australia, the Early Marchers caught four dozen (48) King George whiting.[58] The local paper in the sleepy hamlet smelled a scoop. With a misguided headline that proclaimed 'Men from Adelaide catch *forty eight dozen* whiting' the locals threatened to lynch them.

The photos sit on the pool table. Flat slices carved from the loaf of time, nothing in front and nothing behind. They don't look at the photos: it isn't them, it isn't now.

I look at this structured fraternity ... this band of brothers ... a family of men. They have spent half of their lives and some of their deaths together. There were no rules, no constitution nor agenda. And there were never any blues[59] or arguments, just mateship.

'We never got offensive, just passed out,' laughs Bill.

They are acutely aware of one another in the room. Each intuitively tuned to the other's mannerisms and their capacity to credibly finish a tale. Each poised ready to support the storyteller in case fill-ins were necessary to avoid awkward gaps. They had their roles in the hierarchy. Max Cooper spoke for George. Jamie needed Norm to support and affirm his stories, and Max Ramsay, together with Craig Rossiter, engaged them all, and clarified the essential peripheral details of dates and names. Bill Ditter also spoke for George. Bill was sporadic with his own input. But when he did contribute it caused flare-ups of laughter and much competing to add to what he had said. He sparked other memories and other stories with dry, self-deprecating humour.

Bill is articulate and profound and he generates much reverie and nostalgia. Especially in Max Cooper, who is battling illness.

The emotion in the room is intense. Some of it is irritation due to the physical changes life brings with getting old. Some is sadness for the possibility that it might be their last gathering. But mostly, it is joy. There is a natural ease about them. They are in the company of those who understand them, those they know so well. They hold nothing back. There is a resolve to contribute and build their stories together; a collective determination to sieve through the memories and urge each other on: to remember.

> Coop: 'What about another trip?'
> Bill: 'You have to know when a good thing is over …'
> Craig: 'We've got our memories …'
> Coop: 'Look at all of us, we're gone.'
> Coop: 'It was my world …'

George Collet leans too far one way. He almost topples from his chair. Max reaches out and grasps George's arm with his one good hand—having lost the other to polio in his youth. He holds on tight. In a surprising burst of speed, Bill Ditter propels himself from his own chair and helps Max to return George to an upright position. Once settled, George thanks them both.

'I'll always stand for you George,' says Bill.

> Max Cooper died 7 Dec 2010
> George Collet died 5 July 2013.
> RIP
> Coop and Bosun

29

Pink shorts

There is a bottle of red on the table.

'Norm was just here. He's got some news.'

'Where is he now?' I ask.

She was in no hurry to give details.

'He's gone home to get another piece of paper; he brought the wrong one.'

What paper? What wrong one? What news? Why do women get such a kick out of doing this? She knows I have no patience.

'He's such a sweet man. I don't think he wanted to drink wine with me while you were out ... isn't that cute?'

Why is that cute?

A thatch of tight white curls appears above the side fence. Norm is back. He struggles with the gate. He lifts, pushes and scrapes it across the brick paving. *I must fix that.* He bends a long way down to scratch our dog's belly as she shamelessly exposes herself at his feet, blocking his way. *Move ... for God's sake Molly!* He inches his way around her then ducks and dodges branches and palm fronds that form an archway to the back door. He makes it inside safely. I can breathe again.

Norm had seen Warren Bonython on The Parade at Norwood. He was wearing a suit and a tie and looked to be in a hurry. Norm had never seen Warren in a suit, only in shorts. 'He even wore pink shorts a few years back, you know, like Donny Dunstan. I think Jamie Shepherd wore them too. Not the same shorts mind you (*Get on with it Norm!)* just the same colour,' he laughs.

The pink shorts were probably rose-coloured denim. I remember the trend was part of the hysteria of inexplicable fashion during the 1970s. But they would always be 'pink shorts' to the footballer in Norm Walker. Don Dunstan[60] made a statement when he wore a pair into the South Australian parliament. Warren Bonython probably wore his on a trekking adventure across the Flinders Ranges[61] or the Simpson Desert:[62] pink shorts on the steps of parliament, pink shorts on the slopes of St Mary's Peak. I think the Pink Ladies[63] would support bronzed statues of both men, wearing pink shorts, to be erected on a plinth towering over the intersection of North Terrace and King William Streets.[64] Each year, a Pink Shorts for Breast Cancer Day would be a fitting tribute to two astonishing South Australian achievers.

Norm opens the wine. It's old. It has a cork. Glasses appear, polished and shiny. They jingle and tinkle as they are manoeuvred into position. Norm pours. He flicks his glass with his fingernail and lifts it to his ear. The glasses chime as we feather-touch them between us. Eye contact is made to complete the ritual. He winks at my wife, takes a deep sniff of the wine, a close look, and a long draw before finally saying:

'Warren Bonython wants you to give him a call.'

30

Norma, Thelma, Bunty and Warren

Norma Walker is a feisty, intelligent, articulate woman who likes nothing better than to get the facts straight. She is also the wife of Norm Walker. And when memories collide between Norm and Norma Walker, Norma always wins.

Norma Kelynack Bartlett came to Adelaide as a schoolgirl from Mount Gambier, in the state's south-east. Norma and her sister were boarders at Woodlands School for girls. Her sister hated boarding school and kept running away. But Norma loved it at Woodlands, where young ladies were well-educated and groomed for life. They always dressed for dinner in black velvet dresses and glossy black patent-leather shoes and their manners were impeccable. In Norma Walker it shows. She is a very stylish lady with coiffured hair and a 'dressed for company' look about her. Her warm, genuine smile engages you and her lively perceptive eyes have an ability to hold your attention. The young schoolgirl is still there as the memories dance in her eyes and in her voice.

Norma eventually moved to Adelaide to find work. She met Norm through a mutual friend and the relationship grew.

In 1955 Norm and Norma were married in St Peter's College chapel,[65] and had their reception at Beaumont House.[66] They moved in with Hurtle and Nellie Walker on Penfold Road, Magill until their house was built next door. Progress followed them: vineyards were sold and views were lost.

Norma got on well with Hurtle. She noticed he had selective deafness just like Norm. 'Norm second-guesses every conversation and has done for so long he's good at it, but he won't own up.'

Norm relies on her a lot, but somehow I think this pleases her.

Nellie Walker didn't drive, so she was always around a lot. 'She would read the *Women's Weekly*[67] on how to bring up kids and make sure she let me know about it,' says Norma. Nellie's sister, Bessie, lived in Romalo Avenue so the men ran an illegal phone connection up Ormond Avenue and across the vines to Romalo. That way Nellie and Bessie could talk for as long as they liked on the phone. Norma thought they really didn't need a phone as they were loud enough without one.

The wine industry was a very sociable industry. Norma attended many functions with Norm until the babies came. She was now a mother and the wife of a man who had a very sociable occupation: was a famous footballer, for the Norwood club and the state side; travelled the world on wine business; became a member of Apex, and evolved into an Early Marcher.

There were happy hours, wine weeks and business sessions where Norm didn't get home until late or was interstate. Norma was all for Apex. The Apex wives got on well, but the women were too busy with their families to go along to all the functions.

Norm insists they went on two overseas trips to the champagne houses of Europe together. Norma is adamant she only went once. When Norm went on his own she was three months pregnant with their youngest son, Andy. Norm's mother, Nellie, was sick and one-by-one the three children, Jane, Catherine and Nick came down with chickenpox. Norma took care of Nellie, cooked meals for Hurtle, and nursed the children.

'Well, it felt like twice,' Norm comments.

Magill has not changed much in Norma's eyes. Two restaurants were the first major change in many years. Up until the supermarket appeared, the village was just a smattering of small shops, the post office and the institute—and they seemed to have been there forever.

Norma is unable to drive now and she won't let Norm drive her anywhere. She calls a taxi once a week to take her to the hairdresser or to go shopping. Norma is a talented artist. China painting is her passion. And at times it was her solace. Norm had a fall and injured his hip. Norma hasn't painted since. 'He needs me now,' she says.

∞

A petite, immaculately dressed woman, with beautifully styled hair, emerges from the bedroom. I look at Norm. His jaw is on the floor. He said it had been many years since he last saw Thelma Schubert. This little woman in front of us has certainly surprised the otherwise unflappable Norm Walker.

We leap to our feet. Across the room, Thelma's daughter Sandie smiles lovingly at her mother but remains seated, allowing Mum to demonstrate her independence. Introductions are made and we sit down in the tastefully furnished room and sip tea and eat cake from elegant china.

Thelma Humphrys was 18 years old and lived next door to Hurtle and Nellie Walker on Penfold Road when young Max Schubert came courting.

Thelma and Max worked at Penfolds: Thelma in the office and Max in the laboratory. The ladies in the office were 'older bossy women' and the men were either middle-aged or ancient. To a young girl of 18 the unmarried, older female co-workers were old maids whose lives were dedicated to work. The working day and their lives were measured by the Penfold's whistle. It would wail at 7:30 in the morning to start the day, then again at 12 noon 'so we knew when to eat'; and then at 4 o' clock to end the day. The 4 o'clock whistle warned that blasting would commence at Stonyfell quarry.

Max worked under a clever winemaker by the name of Mr Vesey. He was a man who guarded his job jealously, and shared information and knowledge sparingly. But Max Schubert was tenacious and eager to learn. He sought-out the knowledge in his own way.

When Thelma and Max first married they lived on the Port Road.[68] Returning to Magill was more than Thelma could have hoped for. To live in Magill and bring up their children surrounded by fresh air and gum trees made her happy. As Max's expertise and status in the wine industry grew, he was offered one of the Penfold-owned houses on Penfold Road. But Thelma was happy to be tucked away in her cosy bungalow in quiet, tree-lined Romalo Avenue.

Norm and Thelma re-live the floods of the 1950s. Dates are floated, negotiated then settled. The flood of 1953 washed topsoil and vines from The Grange vineyard into the middle of Penfold Road and The Parade intersection. The Romalo champagne cellars also flooded. Everybody pitched in with the clean-up. The vines were replanted, in diagonal rows this time, to prevent the same thing happening again. 'It's worked so far,' says Norm.

There is talk of fast cars and how Lesley Penfold-Hyland and Penfold employee Rex Lipmann raced one another on Magill Road. Lesley claimed he wasn't speeding, just getting a feel for his new Husqvarna.

Images from a television report of two Asian students who 'raced one another on Magill Road' flicker into my mind. Their 21st-century cars were powerful, built for speed. Their race ended tragically in death. It occurred to me that the passage of time changes little in the hearts of young men.

Sandie and I are now an audience of two. Thelma and Norm have centre stage, and the pleasure they are getting from this rare encounter is palpable.

As a wine wife, Thelma's experiences mirror Norma Walker's: the wine weeks and the business sessions for the men in Sydney, Melbourne and Brisbane. She describes the lavish functions with seven- and eight-course meals and a different dress for every occasion. At the time, overseas trips were three-month knowledge gathering tours for winemakers like Max Schubert and Norm Walker. Max went on three occasions: the first time in 1949 when he was sent for sherry and port; the second time was in 1957 to Bordeaux in France, then Germany and London. In 1973 Thelma accompanied Max to the wine regions of Europe and South Africa.

The sociable nature of the industry versus the sociable nature of the man is up for debate. Thelma describes how Max fell asleep with the hose in his hand while watering the garden. Norm argues that many suppliers' representatives called at Romalo cellars during the day and it was his duty to be cordial and sample some wines with them.

Thelma: Max blamed his sleepiness on the fumes at work.

Norm: No comment on the fumes, but at Romalo he pulled a bottle of bubbly off the line each day to have with the staff at morning tea.

Thelma: [Laughter]

Norm: Put the blind up on his office window at the end of the day as a signal to his friend Craig Rossiter, who was on his way home from work, to let him know when drinks were served. If the blind was down it meant no drinks. Sometimes Craig reached the cellars and the blind was down, but as he walked by it would shoot up, and the grinning visage of Norm Walker would appear in the window. Thelma: [More laughter]

She concedes. The sociable nature of the man wins.

Thelma's parents did not drink at all. Neither did Thelma. She remembers Hurtle Walker gave her parents a bottle of champagne once which they kept unopened at the bottom of their bedroom wardrobe. A family friend and police constable named Armstrong came to visit for a few days. While hanging his uniform in the parent's wardrobe, the keen-eyed constable noticed the bottle of champagne. He took the bottle into custody and happily shared it with Thelma and her sisters. The bubbles went straight to the girls' heads and they ended up on their parents' bed giggling uncontrollably. Well … grandma was a strict Methodist who constantly boasted that alcohol had never passed her lips. She cast her wrath upon the demon drink and having signed the pledge herself when she was 12, made Thelma and her sisters do the same.

I resist the urge to ask Thelma if she ever broke that pledge—granny could be listening.

∞

Sheltered in dense foliage, Romalo House sits on the steps of the foothills in Magill. Below, the Adelaide plains sweep down past the city and on into the hazy blue of St Vincent's Gulf. I poke my nose through the wire cyclone fence that keeps the outside world outside. Washed in morning sunlight the walls sparkle and dapple the green with white and yellow. I remove my nose and walk the fence line, wondering if Romalo House will ever go the way of the vines.

I look for the mulberry tree. Norm Walker climbed the fence here many times as a boy to pick its leaves for his silkworms. He also once had a clash of wills with Warren Bonython, who lives in Romalo House with his wife Bunty.

Warren, a trekking adventurer and active environmentalist, happened upon a young Norm Walker cutting down a pine tree in Ormond Avenue. The tree was for the Magill primary school Christmas celebrations. It was a task Norm inherited from his dad, Hurtle, who provided a tree for the school each year. Norm finished the task. But Warren wasn't happy.

Outside the stately wrought-iron entrance gates, modern wheelie bins look at odds with the setting. I walk the winding driveway, on high alert for the Baskerville hounds that may be lurking in the undergrowth, and muse over what I might leave with. I know who Warren is and what he looks like. He almost ran me down once. He was coming from the post office in Pepper Street, driving a small gold car at a speed that matched his age. For a man of 92 his reflexes and skill behind the wheel that day were astonishing. I was walking on the narrow road to avoid the drooping foliage along the footpath, weaving my way in and out of parked cars, when I stepped out a little too far. He took evasive action and flashed by without a second glance.

The name 'Bunty' intrigues me. I have never met her but I could probably start a conversation on her name alone. She must, however, get asked about its origins by everyone she meets. I have a list of questions but decide to use them only if I need to. Bunty is 88 years old and Warren is 92. I will let their experiences lead the way and listen closely to what they have to say.

From the fence line on Ormond Avenue glimpses of the house are visible, but it is invisible from any other point on the perimeter. I had imagined that the front faced the sea, but it faces north, expressly designed to minimise the intense morning and afternoon summer sun. To my right a raised patio overlooks a broad stretch of the Adelaide plains. Bright yellow window shutters dot the glaring white façade, making me squint. I climb the steps and enter the box-like turreted portico. Then I cross a terrace of marble flagstones and stand before the front entrance of Home Park, La Perouse, and Romalo House.

Warren greets me at the door. We shake hands and I half-expect him to say *nearly got you that day in Pepper Street*. He is wearing a suit and tie and his hair is neatly combed over. There are the obligatory sun spots on his hands and face that come with age and the summer furnace of a climate such as ours. In Warren's life they are a rite of passage, markers of the miles and miles he trekked. He is small in stature, shrunk with age, but his movements radiate the boundless energy of a much younger man.

He leads me to a room crammed with treasures. It is organised clutter. Original oils in ornate frames adorn the walls beneath high ceilings. Blue china crockery and colourful statuettes fill stylish, glass-fronted cabinets. Elegant furniture, French-style antiques and oriental pieces blend in the *mélange* of a lifetime of discerning taste. It is over-whelming, but I don't say so. I'm not sure why. I think it is because everyone who walks into this room 'says so'. I feel as though time has shifted. I am in a space that allows my senses to dwell in another time.

Warren sits me in a specific chair. He positions himself directly opposite me, cross-legged on a chaise longue: *the only way to sit on a chaise longue.* He adjusts his posture to make sure his hearing aid is in line with the direction of my voice. Between us an antique marble coffee table holds an array of colourful books.

Warren knew Hurtle Walker and knew that Norm had been a winemaker who played football for the Norwood club. Other than that he saw Norm only on the rare occasion around Magill or in Norwood. Warren had walked many miles with Jamie Shepherd, an Early Marcher and a friend of Norm's. I do not mention the Christmas tree incident and leave the pink shorts alone.

Warren Bonython walked everywhere at one time. He now uses Bunty's car to go to the post office or deliver the wheelie bins to the front gate. To say he walked everywhere is an understatement. He explored the Flinders Ranges, the Simpson Desert, Lake Eyre[69] and the Gammon Ranges[70] on foot. At the age of 50 he trekked to the end of the Flinders Ranges, celebrating with a bottle of Grange Hermitage when he got there. He marked another birthday in much the same way. At 88 years of age he trekked the length of the Gammon Ranges.

The door opens and a lady in a housecoat enters the room—warm and lovely. It's Bunty. We stand. Warren helps her to a spot on the lounge beside him.

I introduce myself and we sit. She explains that the in-home carer has just helped her take a shower and she apologises for the housecoat. Warren can still hear me but now he can't hear Bunty. He wriggles around on the lounge until his hearing aid picks up the sound waves at the point where the words meet. It is now a three-way conversation.

They speak of their son, who has the Volvo franchise for the Asia-Pacific region and lives in Thailand with his wife. Her hobby is photography and she takes beautiful photographs, which they show me in the books on the coffee table. The photos *are* beautiful. The work is dedicated to her in-laws and the images reflect the eye of a true artist.

Bunty has lived in Romalo House for 83 years. As a small child she had a Scottish nanny. The nanny would call her 'wee bantam' in a thick Scottish brogue, which to the ears of young Australian children was interpreted as 'wee bunty'. The name Bunty and its origins have stayed with her to this day and I wonder how many times the story has been told.

The Longbottoms were the first owners of the property. It was then called Home Park. Warren tells the story of Reverend Longbottom. The good reverend, while on his way to Perth,[71] was shipwrecked in South Australia's Coorong.[72] This energetic man of faith survived the shipwreck and walked all the way to the city of Adelaide.

There was a great shortage of clergymen in South Australia at the time, so local parishioners latched onto Longbottom and didn't let go. A resident clergyman was a prerequisite for the consecration of a church. The parishioners all but kidnapped the reverend. Consequently, their church, St George's of Magill, was the first Anglican Church to be consecrated in South Australia.

Bunty and Warren knew the Schuberts well; Thelma Schubert is still a close neighbour in Romalo Avenue. Max Schubert came to Bunty's aid one day when she was running around the streets chasing a black horse. She had borrowed the horse from someone who was happy for her to look after it while her children learned to ride. What the owner did not to tell her was that this black horse was adept at opening gates. Max and Bunty tracked the renegade down and Max managed to get a halter over its head. Bunty immediately returned the escape artist to its owner. She did not want a horse that could open gates.

I look at them both. How dedicated they are to one another! Each listens patiently, exchanging warm glances, while the other speaks. Marriage today seems to be a 'tick the box' experience and is rarely everlasting. Other than church, Bunty and Warren don't get around much anymore. But they have each other, they have their family and they have their haven.

31

Water-white and tickin'

The article is entitled 'The Men behind Grange,' and the interview headed 'Maintaining the Link with the Past.' Beside the photograph the caption reads: *John Bird, senior red winemaker and consultant, 1960 – current.*

John Bird has a likeable look. His roguish smile beams at me from the pages of *Wine State*[73] magazine. The smiles of a lifetime have etched furrows in his cheeks and a network of lines around his eyes. The furrows meet the eyes and you know the smile is genuine. This face has character. Fluffy white hair completes the picture and suits the vintage of this man. It occurs to me that winemakers, Norm Walker, Max Schubert and John Bird, have a similar look.

I think back to the day Norm introduced him to me as *Johnny* Bird. Probably because that was what Norm called him when they were younger men; Norm and I had been talking in the den when *Johnny* dropped by for a visit.

∞

'John Miller's aunty took to the screw-top with scissors.'

Johnny Bird and Norm were discussing how cork is seldom used in the industry anymore. The screw-top has all but taken over. No more corked wine, crumbling corks or wrestling with hi-tech bottle openers. Unscrew the top and out it comes. It is every wine marketer's dream: *the quicker you can pour, the more you will drink*. No more genteel rituals of removing the cork slowly, studying its dark red tip, and sniffing it in anticipation of what to expect from the wine in the bottle.

Besides having a tenacious aunty, John Miller is the manager of Penfold's cellar door sales and winery tours. Norm and I are about to contact him to arrange a tour for ourselves. John Miller's aunty was used to cork. The screw-top confused her. So she reached for the scissors.

Norm offers a snort, and Johnny knows what a snort is. He had time for one, but asked Norm to kick him out before he has a second.

Johnny tells Norm the story of a Riverland winemaker who offered a large quantity of rough white wine as payment on a debt to their mutual friend, Giordano Rosetto. He then lapses into a language that is foreign to me.

'It was water-white and tickin', Norm ... y' know ... carbon. So I whacked a bit of spirit in, fortified it and made it *real* healthy!'

They laugh. I laugh. But I'm not sure why.

Johnny Bird began working at Penfold's in 1960. By the mid-60s he was assistant winemaker and by 1970, senior winemaker. He was happily based in Magill and occasionally worked at Penfold's in the Barossa Valley.

Unlike Norm Walker, Johnny Bird did not have the benefit of Roseworthy College[74] when he was learning to make wine. 'Penfold's ideas were it,' he says. But science and chemistry played an important role in those ideas. It was Penfold's policy to understand bacteria, and they were strict on cleanliness.

Their policy drew on the experience and knowledge of Christopher Rawson Penfold, a contemporary of Louie Pasteur.[75]

Johnny Bird, Max Schubert and Norm Walker shared a mutual respect for one another as winemakers. Hurtle and Norm Walker built reputations as champagne makers that went far and wide, but little is known about Norm Walker's ability to make red wine.

While Max made Grange Hermitage in Magill, Norm made Michael Hermitage in the Coonawarra.[76] 'One of the best wines I ever tasted,' recalls Johnny. Norm claims it was luck, beginning with a few exceptional rows of grapes picked at exactly the right time. Johnny believes nature may have played her hand in the quality of the grapes, but unique wines take much more than luck to create. Unique wines are made with skill and care.

I watch them closely as they speak. Their pride in a lifetime of making fine wines and their attachment to an industry they loved is nothing short of organic.

They relished the art of creating something worthwhile: the blending and the adjustments in the winemaking to suit vintage variations, with no two seasons alike. It was the excitement of vintage, the anticipation of the new harvest and the surprises that nature gives you, like a newborn baby. One year in the vineyard in every bottle of wine. Seeing what they have created 50 years on. And knowing they have captured time in a bottle.

In February 2009 Johnny Bird celebrated 50 vintages. Time measured in vintages not in years: season to season, waiting for nature's surprises.

Norma calls out to Norm from the house. Her voice has an edge to it. Norm is out of his chair quicker than I have seen him move in a while. After a few minutes he is back, looking a little sheepish. 'I've left a Pinot in case you get thirsty from talking too much.'

'Come on, Norman it's after four o' clock,' cries Norma from outside.

'Jeez … I better get going too, I've got to meet a couple of blokes,' says Johnny.

We move outside. Norma smiles and says hello. Norm folds the walking frame into the boot as Norma struggles into the front passenger seat of the car. They leave. Johnny leaves. I go back inside to clean up and get my notebook. I straighten the chairs, wash and wipe the glasses, then shut the door behind me.

32

Pende Valde

I look at her reflection as I preen myself in the bathroom mirror.

'What question would you ask if you were on the tour?'
There is mischief in her voice.
'Simple ... *Where do you keep the Grange?*'

I am excited. It is not a public tour. It is a personal tour: like Prince
Charles and Camilla, the American Defence Secretary, Benny from

ABBA, the Kings of Leon, and a multitude of other world celebrities who enjoy Penfold's wine.

The only difference is that the helicopters, news teams, Scotland Yard, CIA, mounted police, stretch limos and paparazzi will probably not be there.

∞

The tour is due to start at ten. We arrive at the visitors' car park and are greeted by Johnny Bird. 'Heard you were coming, so I thought I'd join you.'

Johnny and Norm immediately fall into conversation.

'You know it is 50 years last month since you stopped playing football, Norm.' He is still the football hero in Johnny's eyes. Norm shakes his head. 'Is it really 50 years?' He puts a hand on Johnny's shoulder. 'Well, you would know better than I would—I'm terrible with dates.'

Norm leaves his hand on Johnny's shoulder as they talk. It is a warm gesture of friendship that probably would not have happened when they were younger men. They are older now and time has made touching okay. I listen to their conversation for a while and then shuffle aimlessly to the front of the nearby buildings. I lift my eyes and look around. This spot on the hillside is as close to perfect as you can get. Not too high, not too low. I inhale the warm air and scan the vines. A pink and grey galah is perched on a post at the end of one row. By the time I lift my camera, the galah has gone: *what a wine label it would have made.* I look at the ground. The footprints of Christopher and Mary Penfold lie somewhere deep in the earth beneath my feet.

Norm's voice ends my reverie. 'Come on, up this way.'

I follow along behind. John Miller is waiting for us at the cellar door showroom. He is an open and immediately likeable man. His hair has a sprinkle of grey here and there and I guess his age to be mid-40s. He strikes me as the kind of person you need as the face of a company, to present the all-important first impression to the world. John conducts the VIP events at Penfold's Magill Estate. His character and conduct must be impeccable. He is under the scrutiny of Scotland Yard, the CIA and ASIO.[77] A mere traffic violation or legal encounter is monitored. *I feel important.*

We wander down the hill past the lavender and the vines to the front door of the old cottage. I'm tempted to knock.

Christopher and Mary have just stepped out for a minute and will be back soon. Just go on in and have a look around, they won't mind a bit.

Inside the cottage the presence of the past is powerful. But I don't feel a sense of being in a museum. It is more like a movie set where real-life episodes of the past are about to be filmed. I feel as though I am intruding, peering into the private space of a family. A space their lives made.

We are oddly quiet as we move further inside. I take notes and photos and listen to snippets of conversations from the others.

'I used to fox balls when Geoff Hyland and Dad played golf.'
'*Pende Valde* was their motto. It's Latin for very dependable.'

A warranted solid leather suitcase sits on top of a cabinet made in England in 1765. My camera flashes at an Ellis painting, and again at a collection of the world's most famous wine labels. Dr Penfold's consulting room is in perfect order and seems untouched. Glass-fronted cabinets contain primitive-looking medical instruments that give the room a Dickensian hue.

'He made house calls as far away as Port Adelaide and Glenelg by horse and buggy. And he took plenty of Irona wine with him for his patients.'

The cottage is Hobbit-like, built for smaller people in a bigger world. It has the Englishness of cosy comfort, of being tucked in away from the weather.

Today we live large and spacious in a smaller world. Elaine Trimble, the maid, had little space or privacy. Her room is an alcove with a single bed, and was a thoroughfare for all to get to the washroom. Norm Walker looks at the bed over my shoulder. He could not have lived here comfortably. He constantly stoops to fit through doorways which would have seen him regularly concussed whenever he forgot to duck. Christopher, Mary and Elaine must have been tiny people. The beds are small. The main bedroom has a British army officer's field bed. It is a brass interlocked design, assembled by numbers, with a four-poster canopy above a child-sized sleeping space. On the wall near the bed is a painting of Mary Penfold which I mistake for Queen Victoria. My camera flashes and sploshes the canvas with light as her eyes rebound the flare. She looks annoyed. I check the shot. Mary's face is missing. In its place is a glaring pool of refracted light. I leave her in peace and decide not to take any more photos. The chatter continues.

'Mary and Elaine grew vegetables and did most of the winemaking.'

We decree the decorative china cylinder on the fireplace in the sitting room, was used to carry spices: when spices were currency. Treasured curiosities adorn this room which has the added touch of a *Harry Potter* style slanted doorway with door to fit. On the mantle, a candle snuffer sits beside a stiff-backed bust of a finely dressed lady whose Borzoi[78] is resting atop a deer's back. Mary's christening cup is nearby. It sits on three legs. Each leg is a lion's paw while the handles are coiled serpents. Norm notices the handles and remembers the story of Mrs Simmonette, neighbour and cat lover.

∞

Mrs Simmonette called out to him from over the fence one day.
'Is this a snake, Norm? My cat has been playing with it.'
Norm takes a look.
'No, Mrs Simmonette, if it was a snake the cat would be dead.'
She didn't trust Norm's judgement and demanded he drive her to the vet.
'She was very forthright, running into the vet's office yelling *Emergency! Emergency!* at the top of her lungs.'

The receptionist took the cat and placed it next to a dog. Mrs Simmonette wasn't having any of that. 'Don't you dare put my cat next to that old mongrel!' she cried. She grabbed her cat and ran from the surgery with Norm in hot pursuit.

∞

The bust of the rebel and legendary hero of the Scots people, Rob Roy McGregor, stands defiant on one corner of the mantelpiece. Dressed in splendid hunting kilt and fox-mask sporran, he symbolises the connection Mrs Mary's family, the Holts, shared with the McGregors. The Penfold cottage and vineyard are named after Rob Roy's hut in Scotland: The Grange.

'They say Mary is still here.'

At night the glow of candlelight moves in waves from room to room, and glimpses of illuminated shapes can be seen amongst the vines. Chinaware and pieces of furniture have been mysteriously moved about the room.

The old boys watch me gleefully as the 'Miller' tells his tale. They probably put him up to it and I can tell they are waiting for a response from me. So I give them a wide-eyed expression of impending doom, generate a quivering shiver, and plead with the utmost urgency: 'Where do you keep the Grange?'

We leave the cottage and head back up the hill.

John Miller looks around. He points south across the vines to where Woodchopper's Creek once flowed. Mary allowed wood-choppers to cross the property and use the Four Bollards Bridge over the creek without charge. It was the quickest route to the trees grow-ing on the tiers of the hillsides. Once the woodchoppers had cut down as many trees as their wagons could hold, Mary charged them a toll on their way back.

Johnny and Norm take the conversation to a 100-year flood in 1981 when First creek through to Seventh creek flooded. Penfold's Vat 17 half filled with water and Penfold Road was a raging river.

We enter the hallowed chamber. It is an enormous cavern, cut deep into the hillside, many metres beneath the surface. A large image of Max Edmund Schubert draws our gaze to one end of the cellar. We are at the other end with many red-stained oak barrels in-between. I have an urge to lumberjack my way across the barrels to get to the Grange Hermitage collection, where Max is. Alongside me, Norm Walker is beaming as he recognises a photograph on the wall of his uncle Norman disgorging champagne bottles by the old method. He also spots apparatus from the Romalo cellars amongst an ancient array of winemaking gadgetry on display. He slides smoothly into action, turning handles and moving levers.

Precise commentary accompanies each demonstrated operation: 'Six turns on one to cut the wire, one turn on the other.' The machines are as familiar to him as if he had used them yesterday. He pats the shaking tables where eight dozen bottles of sparkling wine were shaken in one minute, and cradles an enormous hand-woven basket designed to hold 12 full bottles of champagne. Johnny joins in and together they explain how the Herkales fossil filtering device worked. Using diatomaceous earth, fossils adhered to the fine mesh screens on the machine. Wine would then filter through the fossils to remove impurities. The two men are enjoying themselves, happily moving from one piece of equipment to the next, until they come to an abrupt halt in front of the barrels of Grange.

John Miller takes over.

When the wine is ready it is sent to Penfolds at Nuriootpa[79] for bottling. The barrels are then reused for the next vintage. Flavours from previous barrels infuse the new wine. The barrels are made of American oak which also imparts flavour. John pulls the plug on one of the barrels and conducts an impromptu tasting with Norm and Johnny. I listen to their complex deliberations. They use terminology that fuses science to nature in a symbiotic partnership to create glorious nectar.

Norm suddenly remembers I'm there and calls out for me to come and have a taste. 'Sixpence a lick,' he laughs. *I should have brought a straw.*

We end the day at the cellar door. The Penfolds' book, *The Rewards of Patience,*[80] is safely tucked under our arms as we sample some wines.

The young man serving us is from Europe. He is here to gather knowledge and experience in his chosen career of oenology. Well, he's in luck. He will certainly learn all he needs to know from the men beside me.

∞

I would visit Penfold's again later that year to raise a glass of Grange in a toast to my son Jamie on his birthday. On that occasion we were in the Max Schubert Room. We ate the finest of cheeses, and sampled the finest of wines, feeling peacefully inclined towards the world. We studied a painting of Max up on the wall and wondered what he would have thought of all that his creation had become.

33

Radish the racehorse

Even at the heavily discounted price, the Croser Vintage Pinot Noir Chardonnay cost me three times more than I would normally pay for bubbly. But he deserves good bubbles and I feel a little guilty that I have not seen him since he got home from the hospital.

Norma greets me at the back door.

'He's in the TV room. Just keep turning right and you'll find him.'

Their home is built in a 'U' shape with the back door the entry point at one end and Norm's TV room at the other. As I make my way along the dark passage I stumble into a walking frame and all but lose the bottle. The frame is tagged 'Return to supplier'. It has wheels and, curiously, two handbrakes. *Does Norma ever go so fast that she needs two handbrakes? Yes, she probably does.* I get a mental picture of her somersaulting over the handlebars in a blizzard of smoke and burning rubber.

The door to the TV room is closed, and I can hear squealing and grunting coming from inside the room. I open the door and take a peek. Norm is sitting in a chair in shorts and singlet. His walking stick is propped against his leg. He greets me with a big smile. The squeals are coming from a large, flat-screen television not more than a couple of metres from where Norm sits. Dazzling images of leggy, scantily-clad, sweaty women dance across the screen in a ballet of cat-gut and fluffy balls. Norm is watching the ladies' tennis. The incision from the operation traces an angry red path across his knee. I hand him the Croser. He studies the bottle closely.

'Brian Croser and I once had a chat on the making of sparkling wine.'

He unravels his legs and struggles to get to his feet. Finding balance on stork-like legs is difficult at the best of times, but it is now even more of a challenge in recovery from a knee replacement. One hand grips the stock of the walking cane and the other the neck of the bottle. He rocks backwards and forwards a couple of times, like a downhill racer with unusual ski poles, and is suddenly up and out of the blocks, ready to go. I guard the doorway in case he tries to make a run for it with the bubbly. He lifts the cane. I step aside.

'I'll get some glasses,' he says.

Beady bubbles form perfect threads in the wine as we hoist the glasses in a toast to his new knee. The mousse fizzes and my mouth prickles with flavour. Norm is pleased. Brian Croser got it right. The cool climate of the Piccadilly Valley in the Adelaide Hills is ideal for grapes. He tells me that Nick and David pick in the cool of night up in Clare, and Max Schubert used refrigeration to compensate for weather conditions.

We become armchair experts in tennis technique as we watch the Croatian and Russian girls squeal 'koo-koos' at each other on every point of a closely fought game.

The knee replacement has put an end to Norm's days of playing tennis or golf. He asks if I ever played tennis. I tell him I played social tennis with a lively bunch of friendly hillbillies from Heathfield, in the Adelaide Hills, who called themselves the Hills Horrors. The group included an ex-footballer named Thompson whom the others called Candles. Norm's face lights up. He played football against Candles Thompson when Candles played for Sturt[81] football club. His name is Clayton Thompson. I remember him as a tall, shapeless man, like a candle, who suited the nickname Candles. It also suited those who used it. Like a candle, it had the strange effect of lighting up faces and starting conversations.

I mention the nickname 'Radish.'

A sports journalist gave Norm the name Radish after he played a particularly bad game of football one week. Radish was a racehorse that used to run last, in a comic strip. Norm's teammate, Doug Olds,[82] was named after the other character in the comic strip, Artichoke. The article backfired. From the following match Radish and Artichoke went on to become very popular. Doug Olds was short and round like an artichoke. But Doug would deliver that ball perfectly onto Norm Walker's chest every time. They were pretty quick, Radish and Artichoke.

Norm Walker played 114 games for Norwood between 1951 and 1958 and kicked 190 goals. He won the club's best and fairest in 1957 and topped their goal kicking in 1955 and 1957, with 39 and 37 goals respectively.[83] Besides playing in a fiercely competitive South Australian competition, he also represented his state on the national stage. In the 1955 state team photo, Norm stands in the middle of the back row, broad-shouldered and confident, with the other big men of the pack. I scan each row. Some of the greats of the game catch my eye: Don

Lindner, Doug Thomas, John Marriott, John Halbert, Geof Motley, Haydn Bunton Jr., Lindsay Head, and Foster 'Foss' Williams.

It's a dream team. *Radish the racehorse ran with champions.*

34

Dingle berry vintage

The tennis match ends. The Russian girl's squealing technique has prevailed. She clenches a fist towards her support group, pirouettes daintily, and makes her way to the net.

Norm says he would not watch television at all if it wasn't for sport. I tell him about an episode of *The Wine Lover's Guide to Australia*[84] I watched recently.

The programme featured the McLaren Vale wine region of South Australia. On screen were two winemakers. One was a large man with black horn-rimmed glasses wearing a Panama hat and Bermuda shorts. He stood to one side of the screen next to a very large half-barrel filled with wine. In the middle of the barrel, up to his groin in wine, stood the other winemaker, who supported himself by gripping the barrel staves behind his back. The man outside the barrel had an air of ownership about him, as if he were extolling the virtues and organic pleasures of crushing grapes by foot. His Bermuda shorts, which were really Bermuda longs, were dark-red and dripping with wine.

The man in the barrel was shorter with a slight build and a grand, handlebar moustache. He had a pair of short, tight, white, turning red, SANFL[85] football shorts. Both winemakers had very hairy legs. The more enthusiastic the grape crusher became, the more the wine lapped against his crotch. He was breathing heavily from exertion and explained that you really needed to get your toes deep into the corners to get all of the grapes. From what I could see, the wine was definitely 'dingle berry vintage'.

Only in Australia, we laugh, only in Australia.

Norm has a complaint about his morning newspaper. It is now delivered in 'flat pack' which plays havoc with the paperboy's throwing arm. More often than not the paper ends up on the street. Or Norm struggles to drag it out from under his car. He preferred the paper to be rolled-up tight. Dogs probably did too. He remembers his dad had taught their dog to fetch the newspaper by rewarding it with a slice of toast with vegemite. Dog logic dictated: *more papers, more toast.* So Rover fetched newspapers from all around the neighbourhood. And Hurtle spent many mornings returning them.

Another tennis match draws our attention to the big screen. It's the men this time. A giant at one end of the court has a cannon attached to his shoulder and is firing high-velocity, green cannon balls at his much smaller opponent. The smaller opponent is in dire need of a suit of armour or an invisibility cloak. We leave the one-sided assault and switch to the cricket. It's a test match. The panoramic view at Adelaide Oval is spectacular: warm sunshine and manicured, aromatic grass beneath a dome of bright blue sky: white on green, stumps and bails beneath church steeples and swaying tree tops, surrounded by rows of spectators in a rainbow of colourful clothing. Test cricket is a visually pleasing, civilised sport that allows those who watch plenty of time to talk.

∞

In 1955 Norm Walker was keen to spread his wings and try new things. He decided he would like to do a vintage at Wynn's Coon-awarra Estate.[86] Hurtle was easing off at Romalo cellars and did not want Norm to go. But it was only two weeks during vintage and he needed to test himself, try it on his own. So he went to the Coon-awarra.

Michael Hermitage (Shiraz) 1955 won all the gold medals that year. Norm was there every step of the way: from tasting the grapes on the vine, deciding when to pick, to the wine in the glass. It was his best vintage. Cool weather and grapes grown in rich, fertile *terra rossa*[87] soil, clean water and a little of nature's luck. The decision when to pick was crucial. The sweetness in the grapes had to be just right. But no two rows of vines are the same. One side gets the morning sun while the other gets the afternoon sun, and tannins may be more prevalent in one row than another. Tannins in grape skins, stalks and seeds can vary depending on deposits of harsh and bitter vegetable substances in the surrounding soil.

Michael Hermitage, like Grange Hermitage, was produced from single vineyard fruit. But Norm still believes blending is best. Excep-tional conditions that produce exceptional grapes in single vineyards are rare. Grange Hermitage was produced from single vineyard fruit and is still considered to be the best Grange by the older winemakers. But at that time it was the *only* Grange produced.

O'Leary Walker 2010 Shiraz is a blend of fruit from Clare in the north of the state and McLaren Vale fruit from the south. Having tasted that particular wine, I have to agree with Norm.

Today, young Australian oenologists, like Norm's grandson, Jack, go overseas to do vintages: in France and Germany and the Napa Valley in the USA.

The Coonawarra in Victoria wasn't exactly the same as going to France, but in 1955 it held the same allure for Norm Walker.

HOWZZAT![88] The bowler cries.

We miss the wicket being taken. Talk too much, leave the room, change the channel for a second, and you can almost guarantee that you will miss a batsman being clean-bowled, or caught, or hitting the ball into the stands for a six.

But that's cricket.

35

Accidental traveller

Norm Walker did go overseas, but more by accident than design.

At the halfway point during a board meeting of Australian Wines Ltd a break in proceedings was called by the chairman of the board. Most board members mill around the bar, but one, a verbose dramatic man with perfect diction, wants 'Hurtle's boy, young Norman', to take him on a guided tour of the Romalo cellars. The man is Frank Herman. He is the Australian agent for two brands of alcoholic beverages: Moet & Chandon champagne and Johnny Walker scotch whiskey. The company secretary, Don Neill, overhears Frank's request and asks if he can join them. Midway through the tour Frank Herman declares, with much flair and drama, 'You know Norman, my boy, when you go overseas I will provide you with top-notch letters of introduction.' Don Neill is confused and asks, 'When is Norm going overseas, Frank?' Frank replies 'let's put it to the board, shall we?'

The motion is carried by the now rosy-cheeked and jubilant board members. Each is extremely helpful. One suggests a first class round the world ticket so Norm can take his time getting there, arriving fresh to get a close look at the latest innovations in European wine production.

Overseas fact finding trips in the 1960s were three-month-long affairs. Norm is in shock. He had only dropped in on the board meeting to say hello on his way home. He hurries home to tell Norma.

Norma agrees he should go.

Besides being pregnant Norma Walker has three children to look after as well as Norm's mother, who is unwell. Norma will also do the cooking and housework for both homes. It would not happen in today's world. Women in the 21st-century would politely, but firmly, tell you what you could do with news like ... *the board of directors want to give me a first class ticket to go and study the wine industry around the world. I'll be away for three months. Okay?*

In preparation for the trip, Norm writes letters to the champagne houses in France, and wineries in Germany, Italy, Spain and the USA. He writes to Louie Oller, cork supplier, in Spain and to the Casá de la Selva, where they harvest trees for making champagne corks. He writes to Spanish sherry maker Gonzales Byass, and receives letters of introduction to take with him from Frank Herman, Samuel Wynn, and from Stonyfell and Yalumba wineries.

He leaves Adelaide and flies north to Hong Kong for a two-day stopover. Next is India: New Delhi, Agra and the Taj Mahal. He flies to Rome for a day then on to London. It is the 'swinging sixties' and the first time he has ever been overseas. At six feet five inches tall, he hires a Mini Minor[89] to take him across Europe. Norm loves the car but feels like he is driving from the back seat. After a few days in London he crosses the English Channel to France and heads directly to the Champagne district. It is an 007-magnitude adventure, but he still has a job to do. His mission is three-fold: find out all there is to know about ice plug disgorging methods; investigate the use of crown seals during production, and assess any new approaches in relation to spill-age.

Norm spends his first week in France at the champagne houses. He experiences the prestige and lore of the famous names and their histories: Moet & Chandon, Veuve Clicquot, Pommery, Roederer, Perrier, and 'that James Bond one,' Bollinger. He hears stories of how the survival and success of the houses is due to the tenacity of the 'champagne widows' who took charge after their husbands died.

From France, Norm travels along the Rhine to Germany. One group of German vintners are particularly happy to see him. They are quite open about using his visit to avoid hosting another group of visitors from the Soviet Union. They did not warm to the Russians, so they put them off by telling them they were hosting a VIP all the way from Australia. After Germany he crosses the Alps into Italy and stays in a town called Asti, where Spumante is made. Norm makes contact with an Italian man who, years before, had been brought to Australia to make vermouth for Samuel Wynn's wines. The day the vermouth maker arrived in Melbourne, World War Two broke out, and the unfortunate man was interned in a prisoner of war camp. He eventually left Australia at the end of the conflict, without having made a single drop of vermouth. The man is alive and well and welcomes Norm into his home.

On to Spain where the 'best corks are made'. Moisture levels and the wax seal were two reasons why Spanish corks were much sought after. According to Norm, they were 'good to get in, good to get out'. From Spain it was on to Portugal and more corks: back to France and Bordeaux then back to London to catch his flight to California.

One winery he wrote to, at random, was located in the Great Lakes area. When Norm arrived a light aircraft was warming up on the runway to show him the winery from the air. They were not as advanced in winemaking as Australia, but they certainly were big. From the Great Lakes it was on to New York and then Waikiki beach in Hawaii.

He tries desperately to put pen to paper to write the report on his travels, but he cannot do it. He makes himself a promise to write the report the minute he gets home. Instead, Norm hits the surf and works on his tan.

He decides on a swim to top off the day. Back at the hotel's indoor pool, Norm hires suitable swimming attire and stretches languidly on a comfortable lounger. His holiday mood and the atmosphere around the pool galvanise him into action. Norm climbs onto the diving platform and performs a perfect swan dive. He plunges to the depths of the pool. Suddenly, there is a tugging around his ankles. The trunks he hired have come off in the dive. He bends double, grasping for the swimming trunks, squirming and wriggling in panic. He finally manages to pull them back up. He leaves the pool and heads straight to his room for a shower. Refreshed, it is down to the bar for a pre-dinner drink.

Norm is touched by the warmth of people he meets on the way. Their smiles and nods of acknowledgement become brighter the closer he gets to the bar. He orders a drink, but then something urges him to look up. Suspended from the glass ceiling above is a view of the crystal-clear diving bowl of the hotel's indoor swimming pool.

Norm's eventual report revealed how worthwhile the trip had been. The ice plug disgorging method took the human skill out of disgorging and doubled the daily tally. The man who disgorged bottle after bottle by flicking corks into a wine barrel every day for thirty years could do 100 dozen (12,200) bottles per day.

The ice bath method doubled the daily total to 200 dozen (24,400) bottles. Crown seal caps were introduced during the process; corks cost five cents each, crown seals cost one cent each. The new method for topping up a bottle of champagne, after ice plug disgorging, was a small mixture of liqueur, cane sugar and base-wine. The old method used over five dozen bottles per day in topping up.

Our accidental traveller returned home in triumph. Savings from the innovations went far beyond the company's expectations. Norm Walker was their golden-haired boy, and the board of directors couldn't wait to approve his next trip. He went overseas once more. But this time Norma went too. Only the brave or foolhardy man would go alone again.

36

When the bough breaks

The savage crack resounds like a lightning bolt spearing the ground. I raise my head, blowing feebly at the quilt covering my face. I wriggle my forehead free and squint through slits in my eyelids towards the light filtering around the bedroom curtains. They swirl in the breeze from the window. Bright sunshine and blue sky suddenly fill the room with light. *Oh ... God, put the quilt back.* It was not lightning. *I wonder what it...* I hear myself snore before my head is back on the pillow. The quilt settles mercifully over my face.

What the hell is it now? Somebody is talking loudly on the answer machine in the kitchen. A weekend without kids' sports, you would think I could get to sleep in just this once. *Is that too much to ask?*

I make my way to the kitchen. All is quiet on the eastern front. No X-box wars, Halo explosions or the aggressive maniacal chaos of music videos. I look out the kitchen window up Ormond Avenue and yawn. Not just a normal hand-covering-the-mouth-yawn but a gaping, lion-on-the-African-plains yawn. When I finally close my mouth, I realise my neighbour has been watching me through the kitchen window from over the side fence. It is an awkward moment.

I am still in my pyjamas. She is already gardening. I pretend to drop something and bob down. After a few seconds I get back up. She is still looking at me. I smile feebly and she bobs down behind the fence. After a few seconds she gets back up. She smiles feebly. I turn away and manoeuvre my head behind the water-well so I can put an end to the neighbourly impasse, and hear the answer machine more clearly.

I stab at all the right buttons without success. The machine is dead. I lift the phone to my ear. It crackles like the sound track of an old black and white film. The fridge light is off and the microwave display window is blank. The one morning without commitments is now ruined by thoughts of the upcoming agony of dealing with people who disguise their real purpose behind the phrase 'customer service'.

The savage crack I heard earlier was a large bough breaking free from the giant eucalypt in our front yard. It took out a power line and the phone line. Telstra vans are already on the scene. The phone line is okay: 'It just isn't working because it is on the ground, but we're going to replace it with a new one all the way to the sheoak trees,' explains a technician with a thick European accent. I stare blankly at him, but remain silent so as not to prolong the agony.

Norm and Norma Walker are watching the goings-on from the verge at the top of their driveway. They don't look happy. Before I can say good morning they exchange a few heated words between themselves then disappear down the driveway and into the house. I leave Telstra to their labours and head across the road. Norma comes to the door and we talk on the doorstep.

She is grumpy with Norm. Their phone line hasn't worked for a few days even before the bough came down. 'I wanted him to have a word to the man from Big Pond. But would he listen? No. He said the man from Big Pond was there for your computers and not the phone lines.' She was clearly upset. The landline is their lifeline. I decided not to go inside to see Norm.

Norma looks fierce, standing in the doorway clutching her walking frame, white-knuckled and formidable. I tell her I will talk to Telstra and explain that she has a medical condition and that both she and Norm are at risk in a house without a telephone.

Norma's not finished. 'He thinks he can do without me … says I'm always crotchety with him … "you've got a mobile phone why don't you bloody well use it," he says. A mobile phone is difficult to use: too compact for arthritic fingers. Suddenly it's over, out of her system. She smiles. Norm is hiding somewhere in the house, probably grumbling about technology and wondering how life got so complicated.

Telstra fix their phone line the following day and I get all the accolades.

'It wasn't me, Norm. Things move quickly if risk is involved.' He had dropped by to thank me for calling Telstra.

We sit in the garden and it's his turn to talk about the tiff with Norma. He explains that whenever he phones Telstra or any other utilities provider for that matter, he has trouble with the recorded options. By the time the girl gets to the end, there are so many he has forgotten what they are. Even though it is a recording, he still feels he is one half of a two-way communication. And when he eventually gets to talk, 'She's not listening to a word I say.' So Norm bought a shiny new, state-of-the-art cordless phone, thinking it would solve the problem. It did not fit the socket in the house. Norma didn't like it. She wanted her old phone, the one she is used to. Not a shiny new one. She would have to fiddle with the new one before feeling comfortable using it.

I told him about my family buying a cordless phone for our 90-year-old mother. It did all you could possibly want a phone to do. After mum had used it for several weeks, the handset began beeping and would not stop. So she went to the linen press and stuffed it between the sheets and towels to shut the bloody thing up. It worked. She could no longer hear it.

We laugh at the absurdity of incompatible relationships with technology. Not realising the handset needed to be recharged, my resourceful mum had managed to stop the infernal beeping but caused a panic amongst her children when we could not contact her.

∞

Some weeks later Norm took a tumble off the snooker room porch that left him with a very painful hip joint. Their children came from everywhere: Jane from Perth, Cathy from Sydney, Andy from Bendigo and Nick from Clare. They rallied around dad and mum and took care of those things that make life a little easier, and a little safer. The girls stocked the freezer and Andy fitted safety rails along the porch. Jayne organised personal alarms for Norm and Norma. I have a key to their home in case either of them uses their alarm, and I receive the alert on my home phone—providing the phone is working, of course.

37

Waiting for the leaves to fall

Swish, swish; I look across the street as he sweeps the leaves. Norm Walker sweeps the leaves every day. I watch him, stooped over his broom. His long frame moves slowly and systematically around the carport. He lifts his head. 'It will be over soon,' he calls out, 'the last of them are falling.' He could be talking about his old friends. But old friends don't fall gently like leaves on the wind: they fall to the insidious talons of old age, defeated by illness and time and gravity, bent and creaking with rust.

Coop was the most recent to go. After a succession of old friends lost, Max Cooper's death affected Norm the most: another unravelled strand in the coil of rope to the past. I listen as he talks away the long years he had with Coop: the fishing, the football, the Early Marchers. I listen, but I will never understand how close they were. I listen, and watch as his eyes moisten with sadness. I listen, but listening isn't what he needs. He needs to get away from falling leaves.

Some years earlier Norm received a letter from a woman named Rose Kerkhof. Rose lives in the seaside town of Port Lincoln on South

Australia's far west coastline. She is a member of the local Pioneer and Descendants' club, and an innately curious historical detective. Rose sent Norm a photograph of a soldier from the First World War who she could not pin a name to—and that just would not do. Attached to the letter was a shadowy, crumpled newspaper copy of the photograph. It showed two serious-looking but handsome women standing next to a serious-looking handsome man who was wearing a soldier's uniform. The caption read: 'Nellie, Bessie and Unknown Soldier.' Rose had done some research and was sure she knew who Nellie and Bessie were. But the soldier was an unsolved mystery. Rose sounded a little peeved.

In written version of a third-degree interrogation, Rose made it clear what she wanted:

> *Was the soldier a relative or friend of Nellie and Bessie?*
> *Why was the photo taken in Adelaide?*
> *Was the soldier on leave or was he just leaving for the war?*
> *What became of him? Who were his parents?*
> *Was the soldier Norm's father, Hurtle Walker?*

It was impossible to tell from the faded copy. Norm established that Nellie was his mother and Bessie his aunt. But dad was taller. This man looked too short—unless the girls were standing on something or he was sitting. The ears and nose look like dad's. But is it the uniform of the Australian Imperial Forces Field Artillery? On and on it went.

After asking and answering his own questions for some weeks, Norm was sure the soldier in the photograph was not his father. He had no idea who the man was, and Rose still had an unsolved mystery.

So in the days following Coop's death I spoke with Norm about going to the West Coast to do some field research into his family's history. We could meet Rose Kerkhof in Port Lincoln and get a close look at the original photograph of the Unknown Soldier. Then continue to Elliston, the town on the coast where his mother was born, chat with the locals about his great-great-grandfather's murder, and explore Chickerloo, his great-grandfather's sheep station.

He could catch up with 'Spot' Guerin, his old roommate from Roseworthy College days. Spot is an Early Marcher who lives in Coffin Bay. Together they could investigate King George whiting, Coffin Bay oysters and some Boston Bay wine, while I take notes.

He drops the broom and makes haste to the den for his diary.

We make plans and set a date. I have to keep it under wraps until Norm finds the right opportunity to tell Norma. When he eventually does he is a little hurt that she is fine with it and 'couldn't be happier.'

∞

It has been nine years since Rose sent the letter. I call the first number listed under R. Kerkhof in the Port Lincoln phone book, and it is her. She has just fed the chooks and is a little breathless. But she listens patiently to what I have to say and confirms that the soldier's identity is still a mystery. Her excitement is intense. The prospect of a little investigation and discovery whets her appetite for suspense:

Good morning, Mr Phelps.

She will park her Red Hyundai, licence plate WIX 328, on the right-hand side of the Flinders Highway outside the Mill Cottage Museum at precisely nine o'clock on Wednesday morning the 21st of September. She has a key to the Settler's Cottage next door, where the photo is kept. We have exactly one hour before the Mill Cottage opens for business at exactly 10:00 am, so don't be late. Rose will begin an immediate investigation into the Walker family and have a report ready for us when we get there.

This message will self-destruct in five seconds.

Rose Kerkhof is a dynamo. Once I have scribbled her instructions across the phonebook, I explain it is Norm Walker's mother's family, the Hamps, we are coming to investigate, not the Walkers.

'John Hamp was murdered by Aboriginals.'

'Yes he was, Rose. He is Norm Walker's great-great-grandfather.'

'I will investigate both families; you just *never* know.'

38

Waterloo Bay

John Hamp was murdered by Aborigines on 23 June 1848, on Stony Point Station at Lake Newland, near the township of Elliston on the state's Far West Coast. The murder ignited a controversy that remains unresolved to this day. Much has been made of the incident. And many words have been written about the murder. The most macabre account had it that John's severed head was found roasting in a camp oven by his son, John Chip Hamp, Norm Walker's great-grandfather. The ensuing reprisal is depicted as a roundup of Aboriginal men, women and children by a posse of police constables and farmers, who allegedly herded the natives to the edge of the cliffs at Waterloo Bay, and drove them into the sea.

Norm Walker's laconic estimation of this account is that it's 'bullshit'. But history tells us that there are always reprisals. The colonisers of the British Empire did not shirk from doing what was necessary to preserve the Empire throughout the colonised world; why would the Far West Coast of South Australia be any different?

Two Aboriginal men, Malgalta and Mingalta, were apprehended in Port Lincoln by Trooper James Geharty and charged with the murder of John Hamp. In evidence, Geharty explained that he arrested

Mingalta on the strength of a remarkable track, found near the shepherd's hut at Stony Point, which matched Mingalta's foot size. Trooper Geharty also claimed that both men had admitted spearing Hamp and demonstrated how they had done so. Geharty's testimony, and the testimonies of several other witnesses, including an eye witness account by another native, was dismissed and the accused were granted Her Majesty's free pardon.[90]

It didn't end there. While walking back to Port Lincoln, on being released by the sheriff of Adelaide Gaol, Mingalta crossed the lands of another tribe near Port Pirie and was himself murdered by the local natives.

In the early days of the colony it was considered murder if a black man killed a white man or woman. But if a white man killed a black man, or woman, it was not murder in the eyes of the law.

And trouble was rife throughout the Far West Coast settlements.

Four natives died after using flour laced with arsenic. They had stolen the flour from the hut of a shepherd named Dwyer, who was suspected of lacing the flour on purpose. He was remanded into custody for ten days then released. On his release he made his way with haste to Adelaide then went on to the goldfields of California. Native reprisals included the murders of a shepherd's wife, Annie Eastman, and a man named James Beevor.[91]

They are tragic tales.

Norm Walker and I will go to Elliston: to where his mother was born, far from Magill. We will go with open minds, sharp eyes, and two-and-a-half good ears, to listen closely for what the wind might whisper.

39

Two for the road

We are boys off to camp. The Fruchocs and Mars bars come out before we reach the city limits. He moulds his long body into the passenger seat and unfolds his legs beneath the dashboard. He is scrubbed and shiny and clean, and smells of talcum powder and Old Spice. Aware that I am watching him, he slowly spreads out a large road map of the West Coast of South Australia with fastidious drama. He is eager to pilot the journey. His excitement bubbles through a long grin that hangs from both ears. *He will be Captain Kirk and I will be Scotty.* I steal a glimpse at the roadmap and track a pink highlighter trail that appears to encircle the entire West Coast. The car drifts onto the rumble strip with a vibrating brrrrump! He gives me a *look* then reaches into his attaché for his long-range, tinted glasses. He doesn't intend to miss a thing, which includes my performance at the wheel. But the glasses are not in the bag. He brought the case but not the glasses. I can tell he is disappointed, but he dismisses it as just another 'pain in the arse' of old age.

I sense something else happening and risk another look. He is rummaging around in the dense thatch of white hair on top of his head. To my amazement, his long fingers emerge from the undergrowth with a pair of glasses. I settle into my role as the driver and ease the car gently to the speed limit.

He rewards me with a melted Mars bar.

In the next four days we will travel 1,639 kilometres and 163 years into the cradle of his past, to soak ourselves in rich and provocative stories.

∞

The Far West Coast of South Australia is a long way away. To get there by road you trace the leg of Spencer Gulf uphill to Port Augusta, turn left at the crotch and then follow the coastline downhill to Port Lincoln. On the way, you have plenty of time to ponder why, in the 21st century, there is no equivalent to the famous, French *Viaduc de Millau*[92] suspension bridge with four lanes of traffic that could float 270 metres above the waves of Spencer Gulf, providing a much-needed shortcut to the vast western coastline of the continent. Distance is probably the prohibitive factor. In Australia, distance is always the prohibitive factor.

It has been many years since I was on this road. It now accommodates speed-charged duels between road trains, caravans, and aficionados of television's 'Top Gear.' Overtaking lanes at frequent intervals are a joy to behold. A pilot car leads the *sortie* while the rest of us trail obediently behind. Faith, hope and trust in the driver of the pilot car, as well as driving very fast, are the keys to survival in the overtaking lanes. That the driver of the pilot car is not near-sighted, far-sighted, suicidal, deranged or criminally insane, is also important. Confidence is relayed to the pilot car by the reflection of an eager line of followers in its rear view mirror. And if the eager line of followers doesn't become confused by the maze of white lines and oncoming traffic, through a sun-filled haze, then all will overtake that one caravan or lone cyclist before being once again forced to slow down to the confinement of a single lane.

The roadside vegetation seems different somehow. The grey, matted stubble of saltbush is not as dominant as it once was. There is more vibrancy and life in the foliage of many more trees and bushes than I remember. It could be the recent rain or I'm just seeing it through older eyes. But the immense, distant landscape remains unchanged and still leaves me in awe of its magnitude. It also leaves me a little baffled as to why *his* early settlers settled so far away.

'Whyalla in approximately three hours,' *announces Kirk.*

I think about a time when it took more than five hours to drive from Whyalla to Adelaide, and jump as a fat insect explodes in a liquid splotch of green across the windscreen.

'Port Lincoln will take approximately four-and-a-half hours from Whyalla.'
Och! Can ye no be more precise, Captain?

He puts the maps away and stretches like a feline in warm sunshine. My peripheral vision is now widening to that of a lizard. By rotating my left eyeball 360 degrees I can see every angle and tangent of his features and every slant and incline of the road behind us, without a mirror: road travel has a strange effect on the mind.

I think about the changes that have taken place in the few short years I have known Norm. Old age has him firmly in its grasp and I can feel it claw at the edges of my own existence. I look at him and imagine what the future might hold for me: sweeping leaves, filling in time, losing old friends.

He sometimes repeats stories he has told many times before, but then so do I. It's not befuddlement and hardly a gradual decline of memory; the details in his long-term recall are too precise for that. The repetition is as much for himself as anybody else. It is how the natural storyteller makes the narratives of life indelible. Makes them endure.

At 84, Norm's health is good. He doesn't seem to suffer those age-specific niggling complaints that monopolise the conversations of older people.

If he did, he wouldn't talk about them anyway. Our conversations are far more interesting than that. He is an avid reader and knows what he likes in an author. His wit is as sharp and original as the day I met him. And he remains pernickety about his appearance.

Unlike my father, Norm has all his own teeth. So I don't need to worry about the shock of seeing a set of gleaming pink and white choppers smiling back at me from a glass in a motel bathroom, or left on a chair to bite my unsuspecting backside, as was the case with my father's false teeth. It isn't so much being bitten on the behind by someone who is actually sitting on the other side of the room that traumatises you. It's the need to pick up and return the offending grinders by hand.

Norm's hearing has gotten worse, and hearing aids are just not his thing. Whenever he does use them he fiddles and curses at them while they screech in protest, with feedback. Today, as we sail along our way, his hearing aids are sitting on a dresser back in Magill; but he is an expert at second-guessing conversations without aids, if I can put it that way. For it to work, however, he needs you to look at him when you speak.

Now, if I take my eyes off the road to look at him so he can *see* what I'm saying, he will give me a look for not watching the road. So instead, when it is my turn in the conversation, I bellow into the concave hollow of the windscreen using it like the cone of a loud-speaker. And after four days of this I will lose my voice.

He begins a conversation with a tale from the Early Marchers' days. And, as always, there are nicknames to protect the guilty.

'Spanner, why did you call him Spanner?'
'It had something to do with loose nuts.'

I can only imagine.

Spanner wasn't much of fisherman. He was more of a bush tucker man. He liked to think he was one with nature when it came to culinary delights in the wild.

A fish split down the middle became a mouth organ as he attacked the roe through the cavity in the underbelly; or he would throw 'un-skun' rabbits onto the coals of a campfire, to cook them native style.

Each Early Marcher contributed to the booty for every trip: mutton and prawns from Spot in Coffin Bay; beer, courtesy of Coop, natu-rally; Norm drew enough wine to inebriate a small country from one of the vats up at the winery. Someone else, who was nickname-less, brought the magazines for those who 'wanted to go to bed early.'

'Who did?'
'What?'
'Who brought the magazines?'
'What?'
'WHAT KIND OF MAGAZINES?'
'What?'

'IT DOESN'T MATTER, IT'S NOT IMPORTANT.'

'Okay.'

Ditz owned retail outlets called Ditters' Nuts, so he supplied the essential beer nibbles. It was his job to fill bowls with his famous fruit and nut mix, and arrange them on the communal table to enjoy with pre-dinner drinks. This time the bowl he placed in front of Spanner was laced with fish burley, or to be more precise, dog pellets. Conversation and consumption continued around the table as Spanner contemplated the bowl. Trust eventually overtook caution and he dug in. It didn't take long. The contorted grimace of realisation gave way to a spray of expletives generously splattered with the mush of chewed fruit, nuts and burley.

Spanner now lives alone and has become a little sour about the world and its inhabitants. Norm would like to get the group together and visit him, but he lives a distance from the city, which makes it difficult.

Maybe we are all a little like Spanner: fed up living with so many others on the same planet, one infinite tribe in the global village. Fed up with avoiding all the socially taboo subjects and secret resentments that threaten fragile identities in the 21st-century. Fatigue now has me babbling internally.

A Fruchoc suddenly appears, causing my eyes to cross as it turns into an enormous chocolate boulder blocking my view of the road. He tips it into my gaping mouth and keeps talking.

'I had a Chevy with a Dickie seat. I took it to the Coonawarra with me.'

'What was wrong with the seat?'

'Nothing, the seat was *called* a Dickie seat.'

I was afraid to ask but did anyway.

'What's a Dickie seat?'

The Dickie, or Rumble seat, was an upholstered exterior seat that could take two passengers. It opened out from the rear deck of cars built before World War Two. As for the name, Norm had no idea. His dad, Hurtle, also had a Dickie seat in his Dodge, a car he was fiercely proud of. With Norm and his sister Joyce stowed happily in the Dickie seat, Hurtle would drive up the steepest of hills in top gear just to prove how good the car was. Inevitably the Dodge would struggle, and the uncouth youth of the day would flash by, screaming 'Get that bloody bath heater off the road.' Some things never change. Hurtle gave chase but never managed to catch them.

We pass the Lochiel salt flats in a pink haze. Up ahead a murder of crows is murdering entrails on the road. I point to the gigantic blades of wind farm generators stretched across the far hills. Bathed in an eerie glow of silver-fringed clouds and dappled sunlight, the colossus-like structures become invaders from *War of the Worlds*. We consider their dominating effect on the environment: on the flora and fauna, and the aesthetic assault on the human eye. We struggle for a solution, shrug with indifferent acceptance, and then quit before migraines set in.

A small yellow sedan is behaving erratically in front of us. Brake lights flash at irregular intervals for no apparent reason and the little car snakes at the very edge of the bitumen each time the brakes are applied. 'Overtaking Lane 2 km' reads the sign. Intuition tells me to offer our help.

As we draw alongside, I can see a tiny, elderly couple dressed in their Sunday best out for a pleasant afternoon drive. Norm gives them his biggest smile nodding his head all the while. I am highly animated in my facial greetings and mouthing of assistance across the divide between us. But we cannot get their attention. They will not look up. They cower deeper into their seats as we draw alongside. Then the driver lifts a bony hand and frantically waves us on: *go on, go on, and leave us alone.* I accelerate away. It gradually dawns on me that my facial contortions, when shouting into the windscreen in conversation with Norm, must have looked like impatient road rage to the elderly driver looking through his rear-vision mirror.

'Well that was a bit strange. What do you think was wrong with them?'

'No idea, Norm. You just can't help some people.'

The flat plain takes a familiar curve upwards from a small hillock, in graduations that shape the imposing silhouette of the Flinders Ranges. Above the towering acres of earth, torn remnants of cloud formations are shredded across a dusky blue sky. Purple shadows glide in and out of creases in the highest peaks. Colours change by the minute. A blue-grey hue over the saltbush gives way to buzz-cut golden stems of grain crops, raked in symmetrical rows. Here and there tiny white and yellow flowers grow in clumps.

A strong cross-wind sweeps through the vegetation and rocks the car. We are now closer to the sea, and Port Augusta is not far away.

40

Port Augusta

A ribbon of steam evaporates into the crystal sky above the power-house chimney. Up ahead, the causeway will take us into town. Behind, the distant slopes of the Flinders Ranges are now a Namatjira[93] watercolour on the rear window.

Port Augusta is not a town I have spent much time in. Some places get a reputation they never seem to shake. Port Augusta was one of those places; a place you pass through to get to somewhere else. An unflattering colloquial pronunciation of the town's name was the most damaging and unrelenting slight on the town's image. It mocked the way indigenous Australians speak and was also a cruel homonym: *Portagutta* (gutter).

We stop for fuel and a pasty. The fuel turns out to be Go-Gas. I have never filled a tank with Go-Gas before so Norm looks-on from a safe distance. I struggle to thread the large hose to the inlet pipe to begin the flow of the highly volatile fuel. He excuses himself to find a toilet with an unlocked window in case he hears a bang!

The pasty does not exist in this mini-mart that sells petrol. It's all big food: hulking hot dogs, rhino-horn-sized potato wedges covered in a gooey glut of sweet chilli sauce and sour cream, and an uneasy multicultural mix of dim sims with chips. For dessert, enormous mushroom-shaped muffins that have a vague link to the reflection in my bathroom mirror. They did not 'do pasties'.

'We might as well keep going.'
Aye Captain, the red planet will have pasties.

We drive by landmarks at the edge of town that hail Port Augusta from the Whyalla side: a car wrecker's yard with its bent and rusted metal shells and stories trapped inside. A display of graffiti grunge greets us. The stylised 'art' encases the ancient concrete water tanks that seem to have been here forever. The art is at odds with the surroundings. There is not a lot you can do with rust and crushed metal, but indigenous artwork on the concrete tanks could fuse them to the landscape.

Once again subtle changes in the vegetation all around me catch my eye, but the arena is unchanged. It is good to be under a vast dome of blue, edged in distant, familiar plateaus of purple and brown. Whyalla is 30 minutes down the road and I feel a strange sense of going home.

'How long did you live in Whyalla?'
'About eight years, Norm.'
'Why did you leave?'
'My baby brother died, and my mother had had enough of the place.'

I remember my Whyalla childhood in shades of red. We came in the 50s, stepping down from a bus into a soup of iron ore dust and red heat. My mother turned to my father and said, 'You've brought us to hell.'

Whyalla was as red as a punched eye. Endless, uncovered lines of rail carriages filled with iron ore shunted in and out of our lives, leaving behind long shadows of fine red ore dust to colour our existence. It was a tough, unyielding place where a punched eye was easy to come by. Especially if you were a whingeing pommy bastard—*You whingeing pommy bastards can go back to where you came from if you don't F#*#ing well like it.* A peaceful life meant compromise—bending to fit in, which few ever did. Relief came with the arrival of the Greeks and Italians. Their presence redirected the scorn and gave the *whingeing pommy bastards* someone to look down on.

Norm and I would not have been friends back then. As a fourth generation Australian he was establishment, and I, the Irish, immigrant invader. But we are friends today. And when we reach Whyalla I'll find him a pasty and show him around.

Silence brings me back. Norm sits with his fingers laced in his lap, gazing at a spot only he can see on the horizon. The motion of the car rocks him gently. He is in his own place. Maybe he's away with Coop and the boys on their many roads travelled. Or maybe he's thinking about Spot in Coffin Bay and their days at Roseworthy College. The road ahead is empty. The tires hum.

41

The Red Planet

The skyline is all too familiar. Hazy red contours of steel skeletons ripple in the distance. Water storage tanks still dot the hilltops to the west. My eyes look east seeking Hummock Hill—my hill—where boyhood adventures in imagination took place on its slopes—and where *The Phantom, Hop Harrigan, Biggles, Smokey Dawson, The Blackhawks* and *Joe Palooka,*[94] all came to life.

We cross the small bridge and turn left towards Whyalla old town. My family lived in a corrugated iron and timber BHP[95] house in Gay Street, when gay meant something else. I can't imagine surviving Whyalla if the word meant then what it means now. I would have been the *whingeing pommy bastard who lives in Gay Street.* Our house was perched in a row of identical houses built on the side of Hummock Hill. Not more than 50 metres from our back fence, rail cars shunted ore that was tipped into holding bins to begin its half-mile journey on open conveyor belt to the belly of a colossal carrier parked in the ocean at the end of the jetty.

Our front door opened onto Hummock Hill. Whenever the town celebrated Christmas or Easter, Hummock Hill was decorated accord-

204

ingly. From the top of the hill, at Christmas, an enormous star shone down over the main street. The star was fashioned out of light bulbs. At Easter the star became a cross, using the same light bulbs. I cannot remember either display ever being vandalised. Probably because the penalty for vandalism in those days was death then torture.

During the Second World War, Hummock Hill was fitted with solid concrete bunkers with gun turrets, in readiness for the invasion of the 'yellow peril'. When the yellow peril didn't arrive the guns were removed. By the 1950s and 60s, the general feeling in Whyalla establishment circles was that new guns could be installed to keep out the hordes of pommy bastards and 'garlic munching' Europeans.

Norm is a meerkat as we follow the rail siding past tin houses dusted red. It is a world away from Magill. The old Sea Scouts buildings have become a dark plum colour from the uncountable layers of red dust, and the surrounding soil is bruised blue-black.

The Seaman's Mission is gone. So are the houses in Gay Street. The land is now overgrown with devil weed and other coarse vegetation that I don't recognise. We pass the Whyalla Institute and I can hear one last song from my brother's band echo within its walls. The building looks smaller than I remember. But then I am bigger than I remember. A Harvey Norman shop is plunged deep into the side of the institute. It looks like an unwelcome parasite belched out by its much older host.

A road resembling a corkscrew has been gouged into Hummock Hill. I begin a sad, ranting commentary to no-one in particular: hissing and spitting regrets and ghosts into the air in front of my face. *Just let it go.* I look sheepishly at Norm. He gives me a Fruchoc.

We find Villi's pies and pasties and eat them sitting on a bench in the main street. I search for faces and memories through eyes of the past.

16-year-old Denise would be almost 60 now, you bloody fool.

I buy flowers from a florist shop that was once a milk bar. The car is warm inside. Norm tells me he likes to eat a pasty sitting in a warm car.

We stop at the cemetery and I place the flowers on my baby brother's grave: *David Shane Neill, 24 Months.* I didn't need to search for the grave. Some images are etched into your life forever.

The long road to Lincoln stretches out ahead; I ease the pedal to the metal.

42

The Unknown Soldier

Descendants of John Hamp, who was murdered in 1848
'Nellie' left, married Hurtle Walker of Magill
'Bessie' right, married Albert Gigney of Magill
The name of the soldier is unknown.[96]

Port Lincoln glitters in the bay beneath us. It is a blue place where
the sky and the town meet the sea. The road takes us down to the
water; past grape vines and neat rows of attractive homes, with well-
kept gardens, that overlook Boston Bay.

I follow the mission coordinates to our rendezvous with Rose.

The red Hyundai is parked where she said, and she looks pleased that we have not deviated from her instructions.

Rose Kerkhof is a warm, motherly woman. She is also dynamic, studious and vibrant, one of an endangered species that volunteers and cares for her community. Rose wears her hair in the long locks of youth; grey streaks at the sides highlight the bright pink frames of her glasses.

We walk through the garden past Mill Cottage Museum to the Settlers' Cottage. The cottage has become a storage space for an immense assortment of memorabilia waiting to be catalogued before being put on display. There is no room to move. Rose looks under stacks of papers and books and shifts things around in an effort to find some chairs. There are souvenirs from Egypt, postcards, tea towels, bayonets, a camel-pack water bottle, used by the first Afghans who settled in the Australian outback; there is an arcade nickelodeon, photos, books, wooden toys, invented gadgetry and much more. Rose uncovers some chairs and is now looking for a table beneath a land-slide of documents. 'We'll never find the photo in this mess. I'll look for it later and send it to you in Adelaide.' She is disappointed. We tell her not to worry and I put the kettle on for tea. I bring the cups to the table, sit down and plunge my hand into the mountain of paper. My hand exits miraculously clutching the original photo of Nellie, Bessie and the Unknown Soldier.

We are elated. But Norm is still stumped as to who the soldier might be. I have my own thoughts but I would like Norm to try to remember. I prop the photo against a cane basket on the sideboard and take some shots with my camera.

The original should stay where it belongs.

Our time is up. Rose is off to open the Mill Cottage Museum for the day. We tag along and she gives us an impromptu tour. The Cottage collection is world class, especially the personal mementoes of Captain Bishop's family. Christopher and Mary Penfold's cottage in Magill comes to mind—so too does the feeling I'm intruding in a family's private space. But how else can we visit the past?

The life of a winemaker and the life of a sea captain endure through relics they have left behind, preserved by people like Rose who care, those who take strength from the past into the future.

43

The odd couple

The motel room looks like what most motel rooms look like. Norm's size dictates who gets the double bed. I can hear the sounds of the sea nearby. The breakers crash into and out of the wash on the beach. It gives me a sense of being on holiday. Norm heads for the phone to call Spot.

Lawrence 'Spot' Guerin and Norm 'Stalkie' Walker attended Roseworthy Agricultural College, in their teens together, and had the time of their lives. Their friendship has lasted for a lifetime. Spot lives in Coffin Bay,[97] where succulent oysters and King George whiting also live.

'He wants to know if we'd like to come to lunch at his place.'
Coffin Bay: succulent oysters, King George whiting; 'sounds good, Norm'.

We spend the morning as tourists. Walking the foreshore soaked in sunshine, greeting everyone we encounter on the way. Norm is a very social being. He has no hesitation in approaching people. His broad grin and easy manner put them at ease.

His mother's family were among the first settlers on the west coast. His mother was born in Elliston, a little town along the coast west of Port Lincoln. So Norm's rural genes allow him to wear the persona of a local who is very much at home.

We get close to greatness as we pat, chat and nuzzle the neck of 'Makybe Diva', a life-size statue of the champion racehorse and triple winner of the Melbourne Cup.[98] She stands proud on the foreshore of her home. Other tourists oblige us by taking photos with my camera as we pose like wealthy owners of the fourteen million, five-hundred-and-twenty-six thousand, six-hundred-and-eighty-five dollar stakes winner. The pipe dreams dissolve in the breeze as we continue on our way.

On the jetty we are greeted by two young Aboriginal boys wearing bright clothes, bright smiles and bright "good mornings". Norm shows me where he used to swim. It looks like a giant basket. A piece of ocean alongside the jetty, fenced in so Great White Sharks can select their own humans for lunch. A little like the fish tanks in Chinese restaurants.

∞

Spot and his wife, Chris, meet us on the street in front of their house. Coffin Bay is a place where man and beast seem to coexist happily. Kangaroos and wallabies[99] share the roadways and footpaths and lounge lazily in the sunshine on front lawns. Birdlife is abundant and the bay is full of fish. I may have to press-gang Norm Walker to get him home to Magill.

Lunch menu: garfish with home-made mayonnaise, fresh Coffin Bay oysters, and Chris's prawn salad, created with produce from Spot's vegetable garden, is spectacular. Norm has brought a variety of

O'Leary Walker wines. And while the others imbibe, reminisce and catch up, this designated driver makes sure the prawn salad is given its due attention.

We end the lunch with a tour of Spot's plentiful veggie garden, and arrangements are made to meet-up in Port Lincoln the following day.

∞

Our plan is to have lunch at a hotel on the foreshore then kidnap Spot and take him with us to the Boston Bay winery. Every vintage, Spot organises for a local charity to do the grape picking at Boston Bay, making it a unique and enjoyable fundraiser. Norm wants to talk to the owner as it is his son's winery, O'Leary Walker Wines, who turns those grapes into premium wine.

Norm and I are early so we sit at a street café to enjoy a coffee. Between sips and licking lips I sense we are being watched. *Look Norm, see Spot.* Spot is leaning on a verandah post grinning at us. 'You two could be mistaken for an older gay couple if you're not careful,' he calls out. We stand self-consciously and thank him for the public announcement, leaving unfinished frothy cappuccinos in our wake.

There is a line-up in front of the food and drinks section at the hotel's dining room bar. Spot and Chris find us a table and I stand in line behind Norm, who is ordering the food. He turns to me and states adamantly 'I'll get this.' So I leave him to it and join the others. I hear Norm's voice above the din: 'What about a drink?' and I look up. He is half-turned in the line, facing a buxom blonde woman in her forties, dressed for summer with all her best features accentuated. 'I'll have a brandy and dry, thanks love'. She smiles at him, knowing what has happened. Norm thought she was me. Without missing a beat, he asks her, 'Would you like ice with that?'

∞

Boston Bay cellar door and vineyard bring the aesthetic ambience of wine home to roost. From the cellar door's panoramic windows your eyes soak in the rich green of the vines and scoop the azure blue from the sea. Our host is Tony Ford, the owner's son. He makes us welcome and is taken with Norm Walker's presence. The winery produces very little wine, sending its grapes to Nick Walker and David O'Leary in Clare to make it for them. But even though it is made in Clare, the flavours are very much Boston Bay. The Cellar Door Restaurant is now the focus—exceptional food and wine that feeds the body and a view that feeds the soul.

On our way back, Norm and Spot talk about Chickerloo.

When Norm and I left Adelaide we had no idea if we could gain access to the Chickerloo property, with its buildings now in ruins. I made enquiries in Adelaide and at the local government level in Port Lincoln. The property is privately owned, but getting information to negotiate entry over the phone became as robotic and convoluted as interacting with recorded messages.

Spot solves the problem. He knows the owners well: Kim and Caroline of Bramfield Station. It never occurred to us that Spot might know the current owners. Much backslapping ensues. *I shall call him Spock from now on.*

The two old friends promise to visit each other more often, beginning with the next Roseworthy College reunion in Adelaide. Their bond of friendship and respect for one another is palpable. They are an odd couple. Spot the farmer and Norm the winemaker, roommates at college all those years ago. One has lived on the Far West Coast most of his life and the other a lifetime in Magill. They stand facing one another as they say their goodbyes. Spot is really short and Norm is really tall. But until now, I hadn't noticed.

44

Chickerloo

'It's only got one bathroom.' Original long-drop at Chickerloo
station

We are anxious to get underway. Breakfast is in the motel dining
room. We find a table by the window and then attack the buffet. I take
more than I would normally have for breakfast: cereal, fruit, fruit
juice, toast, boiled eggs, tea and marmalade, and struggle back to the

table to start eating. *I've lost Norm.* He's not at the buffet. *Maybe he's in the loo.* I scan the dining room. Norm is sitting three tables away and doesn't realise he's sitting in front of a complete stranger. His head is down and he is talking without looking up. The stranger smiles but says nothing. When Norm finally lifts his head, he gets a shock. I continue to watch as they exchange a few words. The stranger points across the room to where I'm sitting. Norm laughs. I laugh. The stranger laughs. Norm gets up, shakes the man's hand and joins me at the table.

'I thought he was you.'

'Jesus, Norm, he's a bit overweight.'

'Yeah, but you get well-fed over in your paddock.'

For the second time in as many days Norm Walker has mistaken me for someone else. Yesterday I was a buxom blonde woman in my forties. Today I'm an overweight, fifty-year-old truckie. I push the toast away.

∞

We are packed for home. After Chickerloo we'll cut back east, across the middle to the coast, then north to Whyalla. At the end of a full day, our journey home will take us late into the night. It will be tiring for us both but especially for Norm. I must consider him first. As we drive, a plan to spend the night in Whyalla takes shape in my head.

One kilometre before Elliston we turn onto the Loch to Kyancutta road, find Bramfield Station and drive onto the property. A tall woman is tending horses in a paddock about halfway along the road to the main house. We stop alongside her and she gives us a warm smile. 'You must be Caroline; we spoke on the phone.' I shake her hand and introduce Norm. Caroline is a very attractive, tanned and healthy looking Australian woman. Her husband, Kim, is working in the woolshed on the hill above the house, preparing for a semi-trailer to call later in the day for a pick up.

Kim joins us at the house for a 'cuppa' and fresh finger buns. I think about the buxom blonde and the overweight fifty-year-old truckie, and go easy on the butter.

Kim and Caroline are savvy and articulate when it comes to the subject of local history. Their knowledge is the organic kind that accumulates from living within the environments and contexts that created that history. The past brings meaning and measure to their existence in the present.

Norm is unusually quiet. Perhaps thoughts of meeting history head on at Chickerloo homestead are making him anxious. He knows his history too. But reading and knowing are not the same as seeing and feeling.

In 4-wheel drive country, you use a 4-wheel drive. Kim's jeep is not officially a jeep, but the adventurer deep inside all men likes to think all rugged 4-wheel drives are jeeps. His jeep is rugged. And it feels ready to take on the worst terrain. Kim provides a commentary as we drive. He stops at various sites along the way to reinforce what he is saying and to show us traces of the past: indelible evidence of the original coach road, or the world-weary remains of an ancient public house, now overrun by nature. He should think about conducting history tours, and I tell him so.

The recent rain has given the landscape the greenish hue of fine-stemmed moist grass. The subtle tones of eucalypts and the contrasts of sheoaks are never as striking as when they sit in fields of green. Gnarled and twisted lifeless grey stumps and rotting deadwood become works of nature's art on green velvet baize. Glinting sunshine through torn clouds causes flat limestone patches to pulsate white amongst the green.

In a moment too quick for the eye to register, an immense picture-book emu breaks free of the trees by the roadside, bursts onto the track in front of the jeep and challenges Kim for the Chickerloo grand prix. I hit the video record button on my camera, and wish the jeep was now a Cadillac floating on an even keel. Footage of the sky, the underside of the roof, close-ups of the dashboard and a stick-figure silhouette of the emu vanishing into the haze isn't exactly *National Geographic* quality. The emu has gone and it is as though it led us to the gate. CHICKERLOO Private Property, reads the sign. Caroline opens the gate and we drive back in time.

The landscape changes yet again. It is drier. There are fewer trees and the grass now weaves patterns in silver, lavender, taupe and pale green. We clench up and judder with the corrugations as the track disappears over the hill to the horizon, where a faint outline of built structures can be seen.

It could be the scattered ruins of a lost civilisation. Block upon block of chunky brown stone and large round silver pebbles are stacked in cairn-like mounds across the property, sometimes layered into fences for stock holding pens. Or they are strewn in or around the windowless walled remains of outbuildings.

Norm recognises the main house up ahead, with relief in his voice. Its original form is still intact. But his face reveals nothing. Suddenly the jeep stops with a jerk. 'King-Brown',[100] says Kim, calmly pointing at the ground on my side of the jeep. Three pairs of eyes rake the grass. A curious, 1.5-metre long (five feet) King-Brown snake is slithering around the idling vehicle. Kim wants to get out and capture it but Caroline stops him. I want to get out and film it but fear stops me—*where the hell is David Attenborough when you need him?* Like liquid through grass, the snake's polished brown skin glistens as it writhes away with a hiss and a snigger.

We drive on to the homestead.

Chickerloo looks older than the trees that grow in random clusters around it. The front façade is deceptive. It is a cottage-like structure that could be a standalone dwelling. It stands elevated to one side of the main building, with a higher roofline than the rest of the homestead, nestled beneath three separate roofs that rise behind it. There is a gaping hole in the side wall and a section of the front wall is parting from the rest just below the roof line, holding on by a stubborn door jamb that refuses to let go. Out here, only the land and the trees bear witness to its struggle to remain.

Kim picks up a sleepy stumpy-tailed lizard as casually as picking a flower. The lizard looks bored: *Ah ... what is it now, I'm trying to sleep.* Its mouth is a thin black line that stretches from jawbone to jawbone. Two holes provide nostrils and protruding eyeballs are hidden behind protective lids that retract lazily to reveal beady hazel eyes. Kim lays the creature in the palm of his hand and folds it gently into the shape of a bow. His thumb is firmly placed on the lizard's flat crown as his fingers curl the stumpy tail beneath its belly.

Kim uses his thumbnail and fingernail to relieve the sleepy of a life-threatening tick that has burrowed deep into its side. How Kim saw it in the first place, which prompted him to pick the creature up, is beyond me. The tick is so tiny. I ask if this is all a set-up: the emu, the snake, and now old sleepy brown-eyes. The city boys are suspicious. The country folk are amused. They enjoy a good laugh at the thought of putting on a show for the city slickers. To them this is everyday life on the land. Like the creatures they share the environment with, they have sharper senses, and strong intuition that picks up on the changes in the air around them, signalling the presence of danger.

The homestead is a shambles inside. Rubble takes the place of missing floorboards and the plaster on the walls recedes from the face of the stonework like the tide from a beach. The lime-green coating flows and swirls in curves across every surface. Pencil-thin gas pipes hang from the ceilings and walls, and swallows dip and dart from room to room, making us duck our heads. Emus have provided soft, silky feathers for the baby swallows to nest in. One large nest is built atop an archaic fuse box, while another is perched precariously on a shelf above a window.

The window rests tilted on its plinth. Either side, the wall is eroding from the bottom up. Beyond the gaps, thick green vegetation bides its time to move in. We walk cautiously from room to room through solid blackwood doors that look unaffected by the passing of time. In the kitchen Kim tells us about an unusually tall Chinese cook, and about Ellen Liston,[101]poet and governess to the Hamp children. A monstrous cast-iron bath leans to starboard like the Titanic on the stone floor of the solitary bathroom. *You do know it's only got one bath-room* echoes from faraway Chickerloo in Magill. Upturned cupboards, and benches tipped on their sides hinder our progress. We go back out the way we came.

I stop and look into the kitchen once more through the prism of time ...

Beads of sweat track down the cheeks of the Chinese cook. On the hot stove bacon fat crackles and spits in a large, long-handled frypan. Flame flares up and bits of bacon rind explode in the fragrant air above the pan. The harsh cackle of the cook's laughter and the shrill chatter of children reverberate around the walls. Ellen Liston brushes past me to herd the children out of the kitchen. Their footsteps echo nosily on the wooden floor as they scamper ahead of her, down the passage to the bathroom.

The others are waiting outside. We inspect the rest of the homestead.

Norm is smiling again, back from wherever his thoughts had taken him. My camera catches a shot of him beneath a remarkable-looking craggy old tree—his grandmother, Sarah Hamp, probably climbed it as a child. The large skull of a stag with long, perfectly formed antlers is lying on the ground nearby. It is a trophy from the homestead living room. Norm places the skull on top of his head and becomes a fearsome, but grinning, tribal war chief. We make our way towards a hulking stone structure standing at a distance behind the house.

The solid sentinel faces out over dense scrubland. It is a perfect place to sit and reflect. It is a long-drop toilet. A structure that lays claim to the saying *built like a brick outhouse.* But instead of brick it's made of large, hand-cut, stone blocks. This is a convenience for all eternity. After seeing one King Brown snake earlier in the day, and knowing how attracted red-back spiders[102] are to toilet seats, I can't comprehend what it must have been like to make one's way down here in the black of night, with just a hurricane lamp, bravado born of necessity, and a 'Wee Willie Winkie' nightcap on one's head.

∞

Our time is up. Kim needs to return to Bramfield for the loading of a large semi-trailer. Caroline will be our guide to the township of Elliston and points of interest at Waterloo Bay.

As we drive, the talk turns to murder.

The alleged massacre of Aboriginal men women and children, in reprisal for the murder of Norm Walker's great-grandfather, John Hamp, gave birth to myths and opinions that are still being debated 164 years on. Many newspapers have been sold on the back of this story. Books have been written and court action threatened to repudiate it. And white Australia has come face to face with entrenched demons that keep resurfacing, in light of it. Could it possibly have happened? Could it? Most of what has been written comes from elsewhere: far from the epicentre where local people are born into the story and give birth to children who will inherit the story.

Aboriginal people did not record events in writing. Their history, meaningful events and myths and legends of the Dreamtime, live on from generation to generation in the stories they tell. So if myth, legend and hearsay leave an indelible residue through time, then why is truth so elusive? Is it because the residue of truth is always subjective —true from the perspective of each storyteller?

Kim recalls one such story.

He was a very young boy at the time. It was night and he was supposed to be asleep in the back seat of the car. His Mum and a much older man were talking as they rode along. The man said that before his grandfather died he told him the story of the Waterloo Bay incident. His grandfather claimed he took part in the reprisal and that those involved made a pact never to speak of it. He said attacks on the settlers were incited by lonely shepherds who had become involved with Aboriginal women.

We drop Kim at home and Caroline takes us into Elliston. She drives us to Hamp Lake, which was the Aboriginal people's en-campment during the time of the alleged massacre. The salt lake is a grey, barren place that offers the imagination nothing. Questions churn in my mind. Why call it Hamp Lake? He was killed many miles away at Lake Newland. Is the lake a memorial to the death of John Hamp alone, or is it a reminder, a place of warning? An intuitive home-grown notion of what may have occurred still echoes in the township to this day. The speculation is that Aboriginal men, women and children were killed at the lake and their bodies thrown from the cliffs at Waterloo Bay.

We turn away from bleak Hamp Lake and drive to Waterloo Bay. We stand silently on the cliffs above the sea. Below is Little Bay, generally considered to be where the massacre would have happened. Low-growing saltbush across an open space of flat land offers wide access from Hamp Lake to the cliff top overlooking Little Bay. I look down. A swollen surge of ice-blue water agitates and spills into the small bay in bubbling white foam. I watch the infinite flow of waves crashing against the silent walls of stone: grinding them down in formless ravages of time. Vivid dark-red succulents and small clumps of purple and yellow flowers cling to the stone face of the cliff.

But the sea tells no tales.

∞

'You okay, Norm?
'Yeah, yeah … I'm right.'
'We can stay the night in Whyalla.'
'No … no, keep going, I feel good.'
He is preoccupied with his thoughts.
'Harry Hamp,' he says suddenly. The glow of the dashboard illuminates the satisfied grin on his face. 'The unknown soldier is Harry Hamp'.

Harry Hamp lived for a time with Hurtle and Nellie Walker at Chickerloo in Magill. Harry's sister, Sarah, Norm's grandmother, also lived there at the time.

Norm recalls his great-uncle Harry slept in a lean-to built onto the side of the house. Harry had a shoemaker's last and fixed the children's shoes for school. They were always polished to a mirror shine, like only an old ex-soldier could do. Norm looks happy as the memory glows. Nellie and Bessie had their photo taken with their uncle Harry.

45

Perfect moon

The setting sun leaves a pink flush in the sky and a fiery glow in the trees. As day becomes night, deep blue seeped in pink becomes a wine-coloured palette above me. A perfect moon is a pearl hanging over the hills behind me. The air is so clear and the moon so big I can see craters on its surface. And all around are specks of moon dust in black velvet. I'm high up on the tiers above Magill. Penfold's vines shimmer in the moonlight. Tomorrow wine lovers will tour the winery, listen to its history and taste its wine. Tonight, it sits silent and serene, timeless and majestic, its giant chimney an infinitely long moon-shadow across the landscape.

Up here is a good place to muse. The dogs are off doing the things that dogs do as I listen to the sounds of the night. My senses lift on the breeze and I hear every tick and rustle in the undergrowth. I dream myself into the black sky and unfold a poet's wings:[103]

Homes thrust upon the hillside
Embedded
A misty veil
Wisps over vines below

Scents of pine and lavender
Soften the frantic road
The plain a fallen night sky
Trees billow black as clouds
Streetlights become starlight
All pushing
The distant milky sea
The sea, the plain, the slope
Suffused in moonlight

Neill, 2013 ©

I swoop low across the vines, skimming the leaves, making them flutter like a cloud of butterflies. Jarrah and the young grape pickers smile up at me. Their faces shine from dark nooks in the vines. Their baskets are full.

I seek out the monuments: the old schoolhouse, the Institute, the Tower, Murray House and Third Creek, as headlights pierce the darkness on Penfold Road.

Across the foothills over the rooftops and above the plains I glide. Streetlights coruscate and criss-cross in symmetrical patterns all the way to the city: row upon row of houses, street upon street. The city glows with towers of light. And in the distance the silver sea shines. I turn back to the hills.

What did it look like then?

Small stone cottages were scattered across the slopes of the sweeping wooded hills, and here and there stood a grand mansion. Cottage and mansion had much in common. They shared a place well chosen by the first settlers, a place of beauty, elevated from the heat of the plains, where the same moon came up from behind the hills each night. It was a place where the sails of the long ships could be seen in the gulf waters, sailing into harbour on the rippling mirage of sunrise. And the bells rang out from every cottage and mansion, to herald their arrival and news of a homeland far away.

Romalo House sits forlorn below me. Bunty and Warren have gone. Their peaceful haven is to be sold. Local politicians have vowed to see it preserved for future generations, and we, the voters, will keep them to their word.

The images fade and I open my eyes.

The dogs are back. Molly is panting on the bench beside me and Pip is in my lap. I take their leads and let them walk me down the hill, down Ormond Avenue to my home on the corner, where my family is tucked safely inside the house that Hurtle built.

46

Under this corner of the sky

It's a quiet Sunday morning in Magill, warm and peaceful under this corner of the sky. The traffic has taken the morning off and the air is clear and clean. But I'm about to change all that. The unwritten law *never start your lawnmower before 10 o'clock on a Sunday morning* is about to be broken.

The old mower coughs and rattles and leaps into the air with each frantic pull of the cord ... *come on ... come on you bas ...* it suddenly fires and I scramble in panic to open the throttle, urging it along before it conks out. Smoke billows. *Yes ... yes my pretty ... come on ...* I laugh maniacally as the forever-faithful Briggs and Stratton motor erupts into life.

The pacers give me a look of disgust as they trundle past the grassy verge. I keep my head down, hat pulled low, and avoid further eye contact. My blatant disregard for peace and quiet has labelled me a tribal outcast. To make matters worse, the shattering of the Sunday morning silence has caused a domino effect across the neighbourhood, where owners of whipper snippers, mowers, blowers and chain saws, have been lurking in the shadows waiting for someone else to break the rule.

I finish my side of the street and cross Ormond Avenue to give Norm's grass a quick trim. Norma is in the kitchen and Norm is in the den. Andy is in Bendigo, Jane is in Perth and Cathy is in Sydney. Nick and his wife Merrilyn are in Ireland and their son Jack is doing a vintage somewhere in France. I'm now up to date on the whereabouts of the Walkers. My family are in the garden with our dogs, enjoying the sunshine, and I'm about to join them.

The mower dies gently as fuel drains from the feed line: silence. The other neighbourhood noisemakers cut their motors the instant I do. I take a shower and head outdoors again.

The dogs prance silently to the gate. Why aren't they barking? The tip of a walking cane pokes through the gap as the gate opens, and a flash of white hair shines down from above. It's Norm.

'I had no idea you were cutting my grass,' he says. 'I thought it was a helicopter.' *I must get the mower serviced.*

'Been watching the cricket, Norm?'
'Yes, when I wasn't falling asleep.'

Norm relives the bits of the game he did see. How Australia was 'getting thrashed' then fought back with high batting scores from a player called Cowan and the captain um ... Michael ... ah ... 'Taylor!' I chip in. No, not Taylor, Michael Taylor was a past football captain for Norwood. My daughter knows. 'It's Clarke, Michael Clarke—he's gorgeous'. Of course he is. To us he's a sportsman; to Maia he's a heart-throb.

I watch Norm as he chats with my family. He is the storyteller. So what if he stumbles on a name or two? He always persists until he gets it right. And waiting for him to get it right is never boring. He fills the gaps with jibes about getting old. He doesn't tell too many sad tales, but when he does they inevitably end up funny anyway. He makes the children laugh at his antics on the day his sister Joyce tried to pull him aboard a horse called Prince, a horse that wanted nothing to do with him. Prince bucked and writhed and kicked the air all the way to the finish line during the 'pick-up' race at a gymkhana held on St Bernard's Road at Glen Norris oval '... no ... Glen Lorris ... um ... Glenroy ...' he looks at me and the children laugh. 'That's it ... it was Roy... Glenroy,' he grins.

Ethan darts off with the dogs to lose himself in an adventure of the imagination. Maia returns to her sketch-pad and Norm is now telling my wife the story of the two blocks of land his father bought for him and his sister Joyce on Penfold Road. They cost 90 pounds each in the early 1940s. 'That's about $180 each, today'. Norm cleared grape vines and planted trees on his, and Joyce kept 'that bloody horse' on hers.

I think about the way things are now, since our adventure began. I think about the house and the vision of the lady in the garden that started it all. I think about the Early Marchers and the elderly residents of Magill I have met, and whose company I have enjoyed, and how my perceptions of older people have changed. I think about Norm and Norma and their children scattered far and wide. I think about Chickerloo and the Far West Coast, and the tragic tales there that may never be resolved. And I think about Norm's visits to my home and how comfortable he feels here. How he enjoys the company of my family and our dogs and being around the house that, to him, will always be his dad's. I think about how we sit in the garden and talk and laugh, and how it enriches our lives. And I think about the future, his and mine.

The dogs are back. Ethan is swinging on a rope in his tree house; something the dogs can't do. Norm has to go. 'Norma will be wondering where I am.' I get between him and the dogs, who are trying to jump into his lap, and usher him safely to the gate. We stand on the footpath and check the traffic. I watch him as he crosses the road and hope that this corridor between the two houses will always remain open and the stories will flow for as long as he is able to come. He walks easily down the carport ramp and into the house that stands on the block his father bought for him all those years ago.

Norm Walker has lived here all his life. His life is marked by an intimate sense of place that connects him to the past. The past is inherent in the landscapes of his life. It is immanent in the gully breezes that seek out the contours of the vineyards, reaching in to rustle the vines, releasing the voices within.

O for a draught of a vintage that hath
been
Cool'd a long age in the deep-delved
earth
Tasting of Flora and the country
green
Dance, and Provençal song, and
sunburnt mirth
O for a beaker full of the warm South
Full of the true the blushful
Hippocrene
With beaded bubbles winking at the
brim
And purple-stained mouth;
That I might drink and leave the
world unseen
And with thee fade away into the
forest dim

John Keats, 1819

Acknowledgements

To Elke, who gave me the courage to realise the dream in the first place. Thank you for your loving support and intelligent counsel, and for putting up with the sleepless nights.

To Maia and Ethan, you grew up with this from a young age and knew just when to enter the cave of the beast to deliver the hugs and kisses that kept me going. To Jamie, you knew exactly what to say when I needed the extra motivation. As always, I never expected any less than your love and support.

To Dr Mia Stephens, friend, mentor and fellow cheese lover. Thank you for the lively discussions and guidance when things got tough.

My sincere thanks go to artist Moira McClaren for the use of her exquisite sketches from the 1976, *Magill Sketchbook*.

Special thanks to Norm and Norma Walker and the Walker clan: Jane, Cathy, Nick and Andy, for their faith and encouragement. It's been an honour and a pleasure to have shared this adventure and continued friendship with you, Norm.

Footnotes

1. Soft boots made by reversing sheepskin so the wool is on the inside for warmth. The common explanations of the name are said to be either a derivation of the word 'ugly' or a Neanderthal grunt.

2. Australian colloquial term for casual summer footwear internationally Americanised as 'flip flops.'

3. Ned Kelly was a notorious Australian bushranger, an outlaw who wore a very full bushy beard. He was seen by some to be a working class hero: an Australian Jessie James.

4. E. Warburton,1981, *The Paddocks Beneath: a history of Burnside from the beginning*, Corporation of the City of Burnside, Adelaide South Australia p. 197 – Map of Makgill Estate G.P. 408/1855, Dept. of Lands.

5. E. Warburton, 1981, *The Paddocks Beneath: a history of Burnside from the beginning*, Corporation of the City of Burnside, Adelaide South Australia p.197.

6. Pilger, J 2012, *The Drum Opinion* Viewed online 4 June 2012, http://www.abc.net.au/unleashed/4017816.html

7. R. Greenwood & M. McClaren, 1976, *Magill Sketchbook*, Rigby Limited, Adelaide, SA.

8. G. Pizzey,& R. Doyle,1983, *A Field Guide to the Birds of Australia*, William Collins, Sydney.

9. Taylor Blend is the name of a popular, local coffee house.

10. The Crows and Port Adelaide are South Australian football teams that compete in the Australian Football League (a national competition).

11. Port Pirie is a town 220 km northwest of the city Adelaide, situated on South Australia's Spencer Gulf.

luch debate on this Australian colloquialism to describe an English-man: in colonial times a possible acronym for 'prisoner of mother England' (Pome) shortened over the years to 'Pom,' or an acronym for 'pomegranate' because of the red cheeks of some English people.

13. Esky is Australian vernacular for 'ice chest' or 'ice box,' possibly derived from 'Eskimo.'

14. Innamincka is a tiny settlement on the banks of Cooper's Creek, 1065 km northeast of Adelaide, South Australia.

15. Meccano is a toy construction kit consisting of metal components, nuts, bolts and washers.

16. *1844 to Evermore*, is an early, Penfold's brand caption.

17. Australian currency before 1966 was in imperial currency: pounds, shillings and pence.

18. Dillon, J (nd) *The History of 31 Penfold Road Magill* – personal chronicle (p.1)

19. Quote is from *The Real Life of Sebastian Knight* by Vladimir Nabokov: photo, *Boys in the Vines,* the Auldana vineyards circa 1902, reproduced courtesy of Norman Walker.

20. Chico Marx was one of the famous *Marx Brothers*: a comedy trio consisting of brothers Groucho, Harpo and Chico, who made many Hollywood films in the 1930s and 1940s.

21. A. Wynn, 1968, *The Fortunes of Samuel Wynn*, Cassell, Victoria (p 98).

22. *South Australian Register* (Adelaide, SA newspaper: 1839–1900) Friday 27 April 1900 p. 6), viewed online 21/10/2011 National Library of Australia at http://nla.gov.au/nla.news-article56550328.

23. Babies were often named after a previously deceased sibling.

24. J. Thomas, (ed.) 1997, *South Australia Births Index of Registrations 1842-1906,* Volume 11, W-Z, ISBN 0947280 32 4, Endeavour Print, Adelaide, SA.

25. E. Wittington, 1885, *Adelaide Observer,* quoted by D. Tolley in *Wine & Spirit*, March 1985. Photographs reproduced courtesy of Norman Walker and Merrily Hallsworth.

26. N. Walker, 1993, *The Advertiser*. The quote 'big and gutsy' means to be big in flavour and bold in depth.

27. E. Warburton, 1981, *The Paddocks Beneath: a history of Burnside from the beginning*, Corporation of the City of Burnside, Adelaide SA (p. 206).

28. J. Pandell, 1996, *Making Champagne*, PhD thesis, Stanford University (p.2).

29. Ibid.

30. J. Ludbrook and others, 1965, *Hurtle Walker of Romalo*, notes on retirement (p. 9).

31. L. Shea, 2012, *Minerva Web Works LLC*. http://www.wineintro.com/, viewed online June 2012.

32. French toast 'to your health' *Entre Amis*, 2002, Houghton Mifflin, Boston MA.

33. Promotional brochure, 1984, *Edmond Mazure: Method Champenoise*, Romalo Wines (p. 3).

34. Mitcham is a suburb located south-east of the city of Adelaide.

35. J. Ludbrook, et al., 1965, *Hurtle Walker of Romalo*, notes on retirement (p. 8).

36. D. Hibberd, (ed.) 1973, *Wilfred Owen: War Poems and Others*, London, Chatto & Windus, (p. 97).

37. C. Coulthard-Clark (ed.) 1993, *The Diggers: Makers of the Australian Military Tradition*, Melbourne University Press (p. 323).

38. J. Ludbrook and others, 1965, *Hurtle Walker of Romalo*, notes on retirement (p. 5).

39. C. Coulthard-Clark (ed.), 1993, *The Diggers: Makers of the Australian Military Tradition*, Melbourne University Press (p. 323).

40. *National Archives of Australia* – NAA: B2455, Walker H F.

41. *London Gazette*, 16 August 1917, page 8413, position 10, Distinguished Conduct Medal – 4 February 1918, page 1620, position 25, Military Medal – 17 June 1919, page 7644, position 14, Bar to

Military Medal – cited in Gigney, G 2006, *Descendants of John Hamp,* Personal Register (pp.141-42)

[42] G. Gigney, 2006, *Descendants of John Hamp,* Personal Register, pp.141–42

[43] In Irish vernacular, going somewhere on foot is referred to as taking 'shank's pony.'

[44] Generation Y born between 1981 and 1994/6.

[45] Generation X born in the 1980s and late 1990s. Those born 1982 to 2001 are collectively referred to as Millenials.

[46] The Interpretive Walk was erected by the City of Campbelltown council: the information was compiled by the City of Campbelltown and the Campbelltown Historical Society.

[47] U. Le Guinn,1969, 'A Parade in Erhenrang' (pp. 9-25) *The left hand of darkness,* Macdonald Science Fiction, London.

[48] The time in which the earth received its present form, and the patterns and cycles of life began.

[49] D. Watson, 1984, *Caledonia Australis,* William Collins, Sydney (p.102).

[50] E. Warburton,1981, *The Paddocks Beneath: a history of Burnside from the beginning,* Corporation of the City of Burnside, Adelaide, South Australia. The Kaurna are the indigenous Adelaide plains people: the Peramangk are indigenous to the Adelaide hills and the Murray River regions.

[51] The 'last tribal battle' is an imaginary depiction of the battle, based on an idea from *The Wokali Shield Display,* South Australian Museum.

[52] R. Greenwood, & M. McLaren,1976, *Magill Sketchbook,* Rigby, Adelaide, South Australia (p. 50).

[53] C. E. Bonython, 1969, *Brief History of St. George's Church Magill,* St. George's Day speech notes: a slate, gabled roof gateway that sits on a stone plinth (p. 6) Donated by Christopher Rawson Penfold.

[54] E. Warburton,1981, *The Paddocks Beneath: a history of Burnside from the beginning,* Corporation of the City of Burnside, Adelaide, SA (p. 206).

55. The Algonquin round table was a celebrated group of writers, critics, actors and wits who gathered for luncheons at the Algonquin Hotel, in New York, to engage in 'wisecracks, wordplay and witticisms'. From D. Herrmann,1982 *With Malice Towards All: The Quips Lives and Loves of Some 20th Century American Wits,* G P Putnam, New York (pp. 17–18).

56. Port Willunga is a beachside suburb south of Adelaide.

57. Small aluminium fishing boats with outboard motors.

58. King George whiting is a saltwater species of fish that rates as the *crème de la crème* of fish caught in South Australian waters.

59. Having a 'blue' is Australian slang for a heated altercation that can culminate in fisticuffs.

60. Don Dunstan was a controversial former premier of South Australia 1967-1968 and 1970-1979.

61. Picturesque mountain ranges in south-eastern South Australia extending over 400 km.

62. Simpson Desert is a large arid area covering 77, 000 square km in south-eastern NT and parts of QLD & SA.

63. An organisation that raises money for cancer research and supports women with breast cancer.

64. The main intersection in the city of Adelaide where Parliament House and Government House are located.

65. St Peter's College is one of Australia's premier schools for boys. Its reputation is renowned the world over.

Norm, and his sons Nick and Andy, attended St Peter's College.

66. Historic home turned wedding reception venue in Adelaide's eastern suburbs.

67. The *Australian Women's Weekly* is an enduring and much-loved Australian women's magazine.

68. The arterial road that links Port Adelaide, the hub of shipping and industry in SA, to the city of Adelaide.

69. The largest of the salt lakes of South Australia in the north-east region: rarely filled with water.

70. A rugged and spectacular part of the northern Flinders Ranges famous for its deep gorges.

71. Perth is the capital city of Western Australia.

72. The Coorong is a shallow salt lagoon in south-eastern South Australia that extends over 145 km.

73. *Winestate: Australia and New Zealand Wine Buying Guide* 250th *Issue*, 2012, Winestate Publishing, Unley, South Australia.

74. An agricultural college in the township of Roseworthy, north of Adelaide; where oenology is taught.

75. French chemist and bacteriologist considered to be the founder of microbiology.

76. The Coonawarra is a wine region in the South-East corner of South Australia, near the Victorian Border.

77. ASIO is an acronym for Australian Security Intelligence Organisation.

78. A Borzoi is a Russian wolfhound or hunting dog.

79. A township in Australia's premier winemaking region, the Barossa Valley.

80. A. Caillard, 2008, *The Rewards of Patience*, Allen & Unwin.

81. Sturt football club is part of the South Australian National Football League (SANFL).

82. Doug Olds played during the same era as Norm Walker for the Norwood football club.

83. J. Pash, 1999, *The Pash Papers: Australian Rules Football in South Australia 1950-1964*, Pioneer Books, Oaklands Park, SA.

84. *Wine Lovers Guide to Australia,* Australian Broadcasting Commission, ABC 2.

85. SANFL is an acronym for South Australian National Football League.

86. Wynn's Coonawarra Estate is located in the Coonawarra Wine Region in the south eastern corner of South Australia, close to the Victorian border.

87. The *terra rossa* soil of the Coonawarra sits over limestone and is world famous for producing red variety Cabernet Sauvignon and more recently Shiraz grapes.

88. In cricket, the appeal to an umpire when a bowler believes he has taken a wicket, is, 'how's that?' Which sounds like HOWZZAT? When shouted in the heat of battle.

89. Small, box-like, iconic sixties British motor car, with limited interior space.

90. G. Gigney, 2006, *Descendants of John Hamp*, Personal Register, State Records – GRG 40-1 Pages 272–75 and Trial Notes (p. 7).

91. J. Casanova, 1996, *When Grass Was Gold*, J. Casanova, Gillingham Printers, Adelaide, SA (pp.26–27).

92. From an *Air France* travel poster, Charles de Gaulle Airport, Paris.

93. Albert Namatjira, 1902–1959 Australian artist noted for his watercolour landscapes of central Australia.

94. Heroes from comic books and radio serials of the late 1950s and 1960s.

95. BHP is an acronym for Broken Hill Propriety Limited, an iconic, Australian, giant of industry that owned and built the Whyalla Shipyards and Whyalla Steel Works.

96. Photo donated by Mrs Selina Forgie, reprinted courtesy of the *Mill Cottage Museum*, Port Lincoln SA.

97. A pristine bay near Port Lincoln famous for its Coffin Bay oysters.

98. A horse race held annually in Melbourne, Australia, on the first Tuesday in November, first run in 1861.

99. A plant-eating marsupial related to the kangaroo.

100. A 'King-Brown' is an especially large, powerful and dangerous species of Australian snake.

101. The township of Elliston, on South Australia's far west coast, was named after Ellen Liston, who came to *Nickerloo* station (name changed to *Chickerloo*) in 1867 as governess to the children of John Chip Hamp, Norm Walker's great-grandfather.

102. A small, very poisonous, Australian spider, coloured dark brown or black, usually with a red or orange streak on the body.

103. Phrase 'the poet unfolds his wings' coined by Elke Evele – 13 Feb 2014.

www.ingramcontent.com/pod-product-compliance
Lightning Source LLC
Chambersburg PA
CBHW021845090426
42811CB00033B/2150/J